SOD WALLS

SOD WALLS

The Story of The Nebraska Sod House

By

Roger L. Welsch

J & L Lee Co.

ISBN 0-934904-27-8

J & L Lee Co.
Postal Box 5575
Lincoln, NE 68505

Preface

Folklore is a relatively new area of study. It did not gain respect in Europe until the early nineteenth century and it was almost a hundred years later that it began to be accepted in this country. It deals with that part of our culture which is passed on not by sophisticated means like books, phonograph records, and teachers, but rather by unsophisticated means—primarily by word-of-mouth. An understanding of this concept of folk culture is vital to an understanding of pioneer life, for the "folk process" was the backbone of pioneer culture: the pioneers were unsophisticated people and they were forced to develop new techniques to answer new problems. The study of pioneer folklore in Nebraska is therefore a very rich, exciting, and rewarding occupation because of the wealth and diversity of Nebraska folklore itself.

As a folklorist I have always been especially attracted to material culture—folk arts, crafts, and architecture—and in particular to folk architecture. For several years I made a detailed study of round and polyhedral barns in Nebraska. I found great pleasure in photographing and rummaging around in these fine, cathedral-like buildings; their colors and textures are very striking and the technology of their construction need not take a back seat to the finest architectural works of the Atomic Age. Indeed, all too often we think of folk technology as being primitive or somehow inferior to our own; in reality some of the techniques and skills of our forefathers make our modern techniques seem primitive.

When I had nearly finished my barn research I began to look for another form of Nebraska folk architecture to examine in terms of folklore. The sod house was an obvious choice. It is an American form, through and through. While our barns often have European antecedents and log houses clearly stem from Scandinavia, the sod house is indigenous to the American plains. It is a clear display of ingenuity and the folk process; the communication of sod construction techniques was strictly oral and unsophisticated—the accepted test of folklore.

At first I considered a study of the sod house in Nebraska in general, but as contacts began to come in from students, friends, and newspapers, it became clear that the Nebraska field was too big. A few pictures of soddies scattered all over the state are available and several sod houses remain standing in most counties of central and western Nebraska, but the information is too uneven in content and distribution to provide a solid foundation for a state-wide study.

I had once visited the Picture Room of the Nebraska State Historical Society to find some photographs to use in the notes to a recording of Nebraska pioneer folksongs and the staff there had a difficult time keeping straight faces when I asked, "Do you happen to have a picture of a soddy?" They showed me to the eight file drawers of the Butcher collection—thousands of pictures of sod houses, farm scenes, towns and villages, prize farm animals, portraits, dramatic re-enactments of historic events—everything that

Solomon Butcher could bring before the lens of his camera. I borrowed a microfilm of the photographs and it took me a full week simply to scan the massive collection.

The pictures' magnetism is irresistible. The gaunt, desperate faces, buildings that grow from the ground, leave an indelible impression of Nebraska pioneer life. It was clear that Custer County and the Butcher collection would provide the perfect foundation for a folkloristic study of sod house construction.

* * *

Solomon Devoe Butcher working at his collection in his office at the State University in February, 1916. (Nebraska State Historical Society)

Solomon Devoe Butcher was a driven man; it was as if he were a twentieth century man dropped onto the nineteenth century Nebraska plains, a man who wanted to preserve what he knew would be otherwise lost for those he knew would follow. At a time when sod houses were at every hand and frame and brick houses were the rarities, Butcher was nonetheless interested in sod houses. It is like someone today spending his time and fortune photographing new car chromework or development houses. Butcher certainly must have suffered his share of derision; some of those whom he photographed probably questioned his sanity, for he spent many days working his way across the rugged, desolate prairie—which was then actually a desert—sleeping where he could, eating what he could find or whatever hospitality offered him. And all this was for the purpose of writing a history of Custer County—a county whose history was less than twenty years old. To be sure, there had been cattle wars, murders, success and disaster, but history? Scarcely. But it was perhaps as a result of this actual lack of a single traditional heritage that so many fledgling Nebraska villages and counties came finally to feel the need to compile "histories" of their brief existences.

Solomon Butcher was born at Burton, West Virginia, in 1856, but when he was still a boy of four his parents moved to Illinois.* Here Butcher grew up and learned the new process of photography. This was an early example of Butcher's foresight, for photography had been born in 1839 and was in its experimental stages when Butcher took it up.

*I have taken all material dealing with Butcher's life from Harry Chrisman's introduction to the Sage Books reprint of *Butcher's Pioneer History of Custer County, Nebraska,* combined with his sod *Houses of the Great American Plains* (Denver, 1965).

When he was twenty-four his parents came to Custer County, Nebraska, where his father filed a claim on the Middle Loup River between Milburn and Walworth. Solomon Butcher also filed, but went to Wisconsin after only a short stay on the plains. He was studying medicine in Minneapolis when he met a widow, Lilli Barber Hamilton. They married and set out for the Nebraska claim where Butcher once more set up his photography business. In 1886 he began his *Pioneer History of Custer County, Nebraska.* He wrote, "From the time I thought of the History book, for seven days and nights it drove sleep from my eyes."

For seven years, from 1886 to 1892, Butcher collected pioneer stories and took his pictures—1500 in all. There then struck a disaster which would surely have destroyed a lesser man; his home-studio burned to the ground, and with it went the work of seven years. Miraculously he managed to save most of his negatives and obtained new manuscripts from Custer County settlers.

He encountered further difficulties as his manuscript neared completion. Then, as now, publishing was an expensive business and no publisher could be found who would underwrite the expenses of the *History*. Ephraim S. Finch, a Custer County rancher, became convinced of the value of the project and obtained support for the first printing of 1000 copies. Harry Chrisman, in his introduction, remarks that probably neither Butcher nor Finch made any profit from the book, but they certainly deserve our thanks, for their devotion and sacrifice left us a valuable inheritance. Now almost eighty years later no money could reconstruct what was; memories have dimmed and greed, ignorance, and time have destroyed.

Chrisman tells of Butcher's last years and of his correspondence with Addison E. Sheldon, Nebraska Historian, then Secretary of the Nebraska History Society, offering his many photographs and engravings for sale. "Now is the time to buy me cheap," he pleaded, "when I need the money so badly." Fortunately the Society did buy his plates and photographs and they are now protected in the state archives.

Solomon Butcher died at Greeley, Colorado, on May 18, 1927. Later his body was taken to Custer County and he was re-interred at Broken Bow.

In his rolling photographic studio Solomon Butcher rolled over the barren sandhills, photographing all facets of pioneer life and history. Here his wagon stands before the I. N. Butler sod house on the Middle Loup River near Jefferson, 1886. (Nebraska State Historical Society)

I began a detailed examination of every picture in the Butcher collection. For each sod house I tabulated significant features of construction and arrangement, family structure, tools and equipment, animals, ornamentation, and location of the house in Custer County.* I asked various newspapers in and around the Custer County area to publish my appeal for directions to locations of extant sod houses and for people who might be able to tell me about sod construction. The response I received was encouraging.** In particular, Mr. Phil Gardner and Mr. Carl Smith of the Custer County Historical Society patiently and thoroughly answered all my inquiries, however bizarre: no defunct sod house post office was too obscure for them to locate. Mr. Harry Purcell, editor and publisher of the *Custer County Chief,* immediately offered his office to arrange interviews, to find guides, to publish inquiries, to pursue leads, and to take photographs—in short, to help in any way possible. And eventually Mr. Purcell's willingness to assist in an investigation of Nebraska architectural heritage brought us to the point of discussing the possibilities of a book about the Nebraska sod house.

When Mr. Purcell suggested the idea I was more than casually receptive. I have found that my work in folklore is constantly strained between two forces, my heart and my head. Ideally and theoretically my soddy work was to be an impassive and objective scientific examination; I was putting sod house characteristics on computer cards for eventual statistical study and possible distribu-

*The Nebraska State Historical Society deserves special thanks for permitting me access to the Picture Room and the Butcher Collection and for permitting me to use a Society microfilm reader. I also thank Prof. Walter Elwell for assisting me in the computer processing of the sod house data and Nebraska Wesleyan University for the use of the computer facility.

**For their cooperation I thank the *Custer County Chief,* the *Kearney Hub,* the *North Platte Telegraph-Bulletin,* and the *Grand Island Nebraska Register.*

tion analysis. But I found it very difficult to remain objective. My eyes kept meeting the desperate, determined, honest eyes of the Nebraska pioneers standing before their humble soddies. Even while studying door placements and roof types I was drawn to the glimpse of the barely discernible little girl peeping out from the sod house door (see photographs 67 and 68), looking at me with fearful suspicion. I was interested not only in how these sod houses were built but also what life in them was like.

This had happened to me before. In working with round barns I had found it difficult to separate my emotional attraction to them from my scientific analysis of their history and construction. Any student of popular tradition, I began to feel, actually has a debt to both the scholarly and the public worlds, for both in their own ways contribute to the successful completion of the study. To my colleagues and teachers I owe my training, and their constant help and encouragement must be counted a major contribution.* On the other hand, to all the people who have written me, have guided me to soddies, and have talked with me about them, to all those courageous souls who braved years on the Nebraska desert, I owe every bit of information I have.** Finally I must thank Harry Purcell, who

*In particular I thank my colleagues Prof. Victor H. Lane for his unfledging support and helpful suggestions, Professors William Kloefkorn and Leon Satterfield for helping me with the manuscript and constantly demanding clarity and precision of expression, and finally Dr. Warren Roberts of the Folklore Institute at Indiana University for leading me to folk architecture.

**Appendix I is a list of all those who have given me information about sod house construction. This is at best an inadequate thanks, for in reality *Sod Walls* is their book.

provided me the freedom that has permitted me to combine in this one volume both aspects of folklore—the objective view of the sod house as folk architecture and the personal treatment of soddy life.

Therefore I have attempted to combine in this book a detailed study of sod house construction (based on a field collection of interviews, previous studies of the soddy, and Butcher's photographic collection) with a subjective treatment of pioneer plains culture. I have used whenever possible the words, experiences, and thoughts of those early Nebraskans who devised and built the sod house, for it was after all a projection of those who built it and endured within it. Just as the sod house became a prominent part of pioneer life, so also was pioneer life a very substantial part of the sod house story.

This work is dedicated
> To the sodbuster, who had courage and strength,
> To his wife, who had devotion and faith,
> And to Solomon Devoe Butcher, who had vision and dedication.

Roger L. Welsch
September 1, 1967

Chapter 1

Before The Soddy

Visitors to Nebraska from the East—especially those from Europe —often expect to find a savage wilderness, barely tamed, peopled by warring Indians and hardy pioneers, rich with buffalo and wild horses. They expect the Great American Desert. School children in Europe ask American visitors if they have ever been involved in an Indian battle or if Nebraskans have trouble with wild horses in their gardens.

Our first reaction is to laugh at this, for we know that Nebraska is no more a frontier than are the mountains of southern Bavaria or the hills of upper New York. We know how rich the soil is. But to a degree both attitudes are wrong. Our vision is as faulty as theirs. Europe measures in centuries its distance from an aboriginal past and New England too is several centuries from the years of wilderness.

It has not yet been one hundred years however since the last Indian wars in this region. It has not been long at all since wild horses and buffalo roamed these plains. People who lived in sod houses and feared Indian raids still live and Indians can be found who remember their grandfathers' telling of their struggle against invasion and dispossession. Parts of Nebraska are virtually as desolate now as they were shortly after their first settlement.

One of our advantages in assessing our history is therefore our proximity to it; we can virtually reach out and touch it. Yet this same proximity is also a major disadvantage, for familiarity does breed contempt, and we often ignore or belittle our history because it is so close to us, because we think of it as being long, long ago, when in fact it was only yesterday.

For centuries Nebraska's plains were the hunting grounds of relatively small tribes of Indians who subsisted on an economy of hunting and gathering. Though some, especially in the eastern part of the state, had permanent villages and grew some agricultural products, their economy was primarily one of the nomad, following the buffalo herds, warring, living in easily collapsed skin tents, wintering sometimes in more permanent earth lodges.

During the first years of major exploration in Nebraska the Omahas occupied the northeastern corner of the state and the Otos the southeastern corner; the Pawnees held a large mass of land in the center of the state, ranging from the southern border almost to the northern; the Poncas held a small wedge bounded on the east by the Omahas and on the west and south by the Pawnees; in the northwest, holding most of the sandhills, were the Dakota Sioux; and in the southwest were the Araphao and Cheyenne tribes.

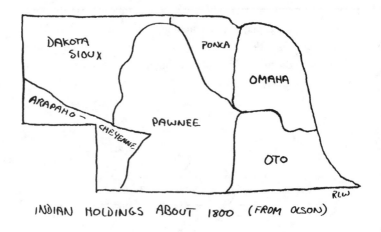

INDIAN HOLDINGS ABOUT 1800 (FROM OLSON)

Omaha earth lodges were constructed with heavy frameworks of timber; obviously this construction was restricted to the wooded hills along the Missouri River. They were permanent constructions and served as winter quarters and home-base for the wounded and infirm members of the tribe during the hunting seasons. Alice Fletcher and Francis La Flesche, in *The Omaha Tribe,* give a detailed account of the building of one of the great earth lodges:

The earth lodge was a circular dwelling, having walls about 8 feet high and a dome-shaped roof, with a central opening for the escape

4

of smoke and the admission of light. The task of building an earth lodge was shared by men and women. The marking out of the site and the cutting of the heavy logs were done by the men. When the location was chosen, a stick was thrust in the spot where the fireplace was to be, one end of a rawhide rope was fastened to the stick and a circle 20 to 60 feet in diameter was drawn on the earth to mark where the wall was to be erected. The sod within the circle was removed, the ground excavated about a foot in depth, and the earth thrown around the circle like an embankment. Small crotched posts about 10 feet high were set 8 or 10 feet apart and 1½ feet within the circle and on these were laid beams. Outside this frame split posts were set close together, having one end braced against the bottom of the bank and the other end leaning against the beams, thus forming a wall of timber. The opening generally, though not always, faced the east. Midway between the central fireplace and the wall were planted 4 to 8 large crotched posts about 10 feet in height, on which heavy beams rested, these serving to support the roof. This was made of long, slender, tapering trees stripped of their bark. These were tied at their large ends with cords (made from the inner bark of the linden) to the beams at the top of the stockade and at the middle to those resting in the crotches of the large posts forming the inner circle about the fireplace. The slender ends were cut so as to form the circular opening for the smoke, the edges being woven together with elm twine, so as to be firm. Outside the woodwork of the walls and roof, branches of willow were laid crosswise and bound tight to each slab and pole. Over the willows a heavy thatch of coarse grass was arranged so as to shed water. On the grass was placed a thick coating of sod. The sods were cut to lap and be laid like shingles. Finally they were tamped with earth and made impervious to rain. The entrance way, 6 to 10 feet long, projected from the door and was built in the same manner as the lodge and formed a part of it. A curtain of skin hung at the inner and one at the outer door of this entrance way. Much labor was expended on the floor of the lodge. The loose *earth was carefully removed and the ground then tamped. It was next flooded with water, after which dried grass was spread over it and set on fire. Then the ground was tamped once again. This wetting and heating was repeated two or three times, until the floor became hard and level and could be easily swept and kept clean.*

Illustration 1

Omaha Indian earth lodge. (Nebraska State Historical Society)

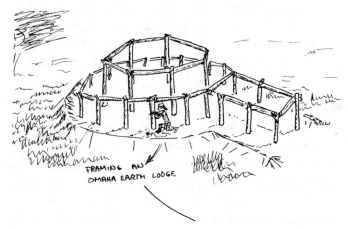

FRAMING AN
OMAHA EARTH LODGE

The Omaha earth lodge may well have provided the Mormons with the inspiration for Nebraska's first sod houses. The Omahas' houses were not built at all like the later settlers' soddies, but they may have given them the idea. A heavy framework of timbers was constructed first.

Then the timbers were covered with poles, then the poles were covered with grass bundles or thatch, and finally earth and sod was piled over the entire structure.

Skin tipis used a frame of wooden poles and a covering of buffalo hide. On the hunting trail they provided a comfortable and roomy shelter and they were easily and quickly erected and disassembled. Once more, we turn to Fletcher and La Flesche for a description:

The setting up of a tent was always a woman's task. She first took four poles, laid them together on the ground, and then tied them firmly with a thong about three feet from one end. She then raised the poles and spread their free ends apart and thrust them firmly into the ground. These four tied poles formed the true framework of the tent. Other poles—10 to 20 in number, according to the size of the tent—were arranged in a circle, one end pressed well into the ground, the other end laid in the forks made by the tied ends of the four poles. There was a definite order in setting up the poles so that they would lock one another, and when they were all in place they constituted an elastic but firm frame which could resist a fairly heavy wind. When the poles were all set, a back pole was laid on the ground and the tent cover brought. This had been folded so as to be ready to be tied and opened. The front edges had been rolled or folded over and over back to the line indicating the middle of the cover; on this line thongs had been sewed at the top and bottom of the cover; the cover was laid on the ground in such a manner that this back line was parallel to the pole which was then securely tied to the cover by the thongs. When this was done, the pole and the folded tent cover were grasped firmly together, lifted, and set in place. Then, if there were two women doing the work, one took one fold of the cover and the other the other fold, and each walked with her side around the framework of poles. The two straight edges had a loop sewed to it, and through both loops a stake was thrust into the ground.

Illustration 2

Omaha skin tipi (Bureau of American Ethnology, 27th Annual Report)

Omaha legend tells that they once used bark lodges, a type of construction that was common among the Indians to the east, where timber provided ample bark.

Illustration 3

Winnebago bark huts. (Nebraska State Historical Society)

Although there are obviously substantial differences between the Omaha earth lodge and the pioneer sod house, there are enough similarities to suggest that the idea may well have been borrowed from the Indians. Wisely, the early settlers were quick to learn techniques from the Indians and frequently borrowed material objects—like the snowshoe and corn—and names, like "Omaha," "Nebraska," and "Missouri."

For years there has raged an argument about the first European visitors to Nebraska. Did Coronado cross into Nebraska during the furthest extension of his expedition in 1541 or did he remain south of the present Kansas-Nebraska border on the 40th parallel? It is at the moment impossible to know for certain, but Coronado was assuredly the first white visitor to the Great Plains region. Surely that is enough; it seems hard to imagine that anyone should wish to claim the barbarous and greed-driven Coronado for his state's First Citizen.

In 1739 eight Frenchmen, led by the brothers Pierre and Paul Mallet, became the first authenticated explorers to reach Nebraska as they reconnoitred a new French territory. They, like so many of the visitors to follow, used the broad Missouri River as a route north and west and so saw parts of the state from the River and probably probed short distances into the interior in search of game and possible riches. The Mallets also went up the Platte a short distance and crossed the southern part of the state by land.

Following the earliest explorations there were other attempts to assess the value of the land and to seek out an easy route to the Pacific. A few French trappers joined the Indians in hunting and gathering, collecting a slight surplus that could be traded for other goods and money.

In 1803 James Monroe bought the entire interior of the continent for fifteen million dollars and that land which was to become Nebraska became a part of the property of the United States of America.

Although there was little thought of expansion into the new territories, there was an obvious need for further exploration and assessment. In 1804 Lewis and Clark, the famous explorers of the West, were sent up the Missouri River and they, like the Mallets, probed the land immediately adjacent to the Missouri River. They followed the River the full length of the present eastern boundary of Nebraska, counseled with the Omaha Indians and wrote copious notes about the land and the people.

Like the Coronado expedition, the Zebulon Pike expedition and its route are surrounded by controversy. Pike originally went out to find the headwaters of the Mississippi River and although he failed in this task, he was again sent out, this time to seek out the headwaters of the Arkansas and Red Rivers. He skirted along the Kansas-Nebraska border and it is still uncertain whether he crossed over the 40th parallel. Pike, of course, eventually gave his name to Colorado's famed Pikes Peak.

In 1810 a commercial expedition financed by John Jacob Astor journeyed up the Missouri and visited Omaha villages along its way to the Columbia River area. The first steamboat to come up the Missouri was a part of the Long Expedition in 1819 (also known as the Yellowstone Expedition), the purpose of which was to lay the groundwork for a system of military posts along the Missouri—the western edge of civilization. The same year, as a result of this effort, the first settlement in Nebraska, Fort Robinson army post, was established.

The protection of the Army and the increasing number of Whites, the inexorable approach of the western frontier, and the desire for riches and souls brought more trappers and missionaries to Nebraska. Visits, official and unofficial, were becoming more and more frequent. Now trails could be established—roads westward. The Nebraska prairie now became more than a desert waste: it became a highway.

In 1841 the first travellers set out along the Platte River, establishing a route that was to see a river of thousands upon thousands

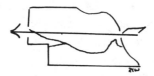

of migrant wagon trains during the next three decades. By 1843 the Oregon Trail was an institution. The streets of Nebraska City, one of the principal starting points of the Trail, were swollen with migrants, trains, horses and riders, merchants, teamsters, hucksters, medicine shows, and Indians.

The frontier had reached the Missouri River. The Nebraska City Cut-Off, the Grand Island of the Platte, Ash Hollow, Windlass Hill, Lone Tree, Chimney Rock, Scotts Bluff, and Mitchell Pass were milestones bringing despair or hope to the struggling "crossers."

Illustration 4

An early wagon train crossing the plains. (Denver Public Library Collection)

In 1846 the Mormons were driven from Nauvoo, Illinois, and they added their numbers to Nebraska's moving population. Near where Omaha now stands, the Mormons established "Winter Quarters" and prepared to meet inevitable starvation, disease, and death. They had only what they had been able to carry with them and they had only a few months to construct make-shift shelters and gather meager stores of supplies. They gathered what food they could from the Missouri banks, hunted on the rich bottomlands for deer and turkey, and built log houses—and sod houses, perhaps the first in Nebraska.

Six hundred died and were buried in Nebraska soil that winter, and their names, inscribed on the Mormon Cemetery Monument in Florence, north of Omaha, are a witness to this harvest of religious bigotry.

The next spring they set out again, staying on the north side of the Platte River. Cass G. Barns reports in his *The Sod House* (Madison, Nebraska, 1930) that the Mormons continued building sod houses on their trek across the prairie.

At [the] junction of the Beaver and the Loup a detachment of Mormons were instructed to make a stopping post for the multitudes to follow on the march to Utah. They built sod houses and cultivated the rich bottom land, made ditches and sod walls to impound their cattle.

As the Mormon traffic began to diminish, the shout of "Gold at Sut-

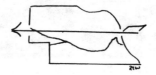

ter's Mill!" in May of 1848 brought a new flood of crossers and again the Platte Valley resounded to the shouts of the teamsters, the bawl of cattle, the barks of dogs, and the cries of children.

Illustration 5

An early immigrant train fording a river. (Charles Nordin Collection, Nebraska State Historical Society)

Settlements then began to spring up on the Plains along the westward route: forts to protect the migrants from raiding Indians (for example, Fort Kearney, established in 1848), hostelries to provide them with supplies and some comforts, and saloons, gambling houses, and bordellos to rob them. Some migrants became Nebraska settlers when they ran out of money or strength, when illness forced them to withdraw from a train, or when a family could not bear to leave a Nebraska grave that held one of their children or their mother. Everett Dick, in *The Sod House Frontier* (New York, 1937) tells about one of the settlers who returned with a broke' pirit from the West:

In May, 1859, D. C. Jenkins, disappointed in his search for gold in the Colorado gold rush, turned his face eastward. Pushing a wheelbarrow loaded with all his possessions, he wearily measured the distance back to eastern Nebraska where he established a ranch at Big Sandy in Jefferson County. There he found the fleeting prosperity which had eluded him in his search for the shining metal.

Mr. **Horace** Davis of Lincoln recalls his mother telling how, from the door of her sod house, she counted in one day fifty wagons going west—and exactly fifty more coming back east. In the second volume of *Sod House Memories* (1967) Mrs. Jane Shellhase of Kearney tells of the optimistic mottos painted on the sides of westward bound wagons and then adds that it was only a few short years before the same wagons rolled back east, bearing the words, "In God we trusted, In Nebraska we busted."

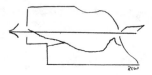

In 1854 the Kansas-Nebraska Act was passed and Nebraska was no longer Indian Territory; it was now a corporate part of the United States of America and, since this was now the case, settlers could expect treatment as citizens in their homeland rather than as aliens in the wilderness. Nebraska was ripe for settlement.

The census of 1854 showed slightly less than 3000 people in the state—many of them travellers on their way through. Aside from Fort Kearney, the only settlements were towns along the Missouri

River, south of the present site of Omaha. But things began to move very swiftly at this point. Stage lines expanded their services, sending new routes north and west, the telegraph lines made communications with remote areas a possibility, and freight lines and eventually the railroad brought building supplies and even more immigrants.

Perhaps the single most important incentive for settlement was the Homestead Act of 1862. Prior to this bill, 160 acres of public land could be acquired by paying $1.25 per acre under the provisions of the Pre-emption Law of 1841, or land could be claimed with the use of military bounty land warrants earned as a part of the reward for military service, or it could simply be purchased from another owner. Under the 1862 law, however, the aspiring land owner could claim a quarter-section of public land, pay a $10 filing fee, and then earn it with his sweat and courage: he had only to live on it for five years immediately after filing his claim. Later, additional land could be acquired in return for the promise to plant 40 acres of timber. The railroads also sold their lands and, although it was slightly more expensive, it was also better land. They imported workers, provided easy passage to the free lands, and generally encouraged settlement, for it was obviously to the advantage of the railroad to have customers spaced out along its full length.

Promoters platted and designed imaginary metropolises and printed extravagant pamphlets describing the wide, treed avenues, flourishing commercial concerns, and solemn universities, where there was in reality only grass. They sold shares and lots to wide-eyed dreamers, who often travelled to the Territory only to find that their "commercial site" between the University campus and the Catholic Cathedral was a set of four stakes, lost in an endless sea of grass.

Everett Dick cites from William Huse's *History of Dixon County,*

The town of Curlew, in Cedar County, Nebraska, was an example of the most glaring and successful fraud of all the fifty or more town sites in the river counties of northern Nebraska. Ten thousand lots were laid out and sold but no house ever was built there. The fascinating map and pictures, portraying the tremendous growth and importance of Curlew, gave the lots a rapid sale in New York. Although houseless, the 10,000 lots brought the proprietors $150,000.

On the other hand, many of Nebraska's present towns are the realization of these commercial enterprises born in imagination and perfidy.

The settlement continued until the First World War, encouraged further by the Kinkaid Act of 1904, which opened up vast new areas of the sandhills for pre-emption, and resisted by the cattlemen who fought the fencing of free range lands and pressures edging the cattle trails further west, away from grass and water.

All of the conditions necessary for the Age of the Sod House were now gathered together: the bareness of the Plains and the hope and ingenuity of the people.

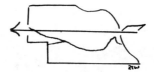

The historical information for this chapter is from James Olson's History of Nebraska *(University of Nebraska Press; Lincoln, 1955), Everett Dick's* The Sod-House Frontier *(D. Appleton-Century Company; New York, 1937), and J. Sterling Morton's* Illustrated History of Nebraska *(Jacob North and Company; Lincoln, 1906).*

Chapter 2

"Made without mortar, square, plumb or greenbacks"

The new settlers came from many diverse backgrounds, and their traditional home-building techniques were just as varied. Emigrants from the urban areas of the eastern United States were accustomed to large, substantial, stone, brick, and frame houses; craftsmanship was careful and construction was solid. Settlers from the rural areas of the East and Midwest had lived in log houses built of loosely stacked logs filled in with mortar of clay and sticks and roofed with shingles; this type of construction also had attained a high level of technology, especially in the construction of corners, where special dovetail joints had been developed that kept the settling of moisture at a minimum and protected the wood from rot and decay. European peasant settlers came from a tradition of half-timber construction, which used a heavy framework of timbers with a filling of mortar or brick; other common styles were all-brick and stone constructions. Roofs were of tile or thatch. Scandinavians were used to log houses, but they were not at all like the loose-fit houses of the eastern United States; the logs used in Scandinavian homes were fit so exactly that mortar was not needed to seal joints.

Immigrants to a new area usually adapt their own traditions to the geographic supplies and demands of the new area. This was architecturally possible in the eastern quarter of Nebraska where there was wood for frame construction, for framing, and for firing clay for bricks. Because of the wealth of timber, the nineteenth century houses in Omaha, Nebraska City, Auburn, Brownville, and the surrounding areas reflect the traditional architecture of the East; but there was no wood on the Plains. Along the river bottoms there was some scrub brush, but nothing substantial enough to provide the necessary beams, rafters, and studs for framing, not to mention siding and roofing. The few cottonwoods along the river banks were quickly used up. Lumber and shingles hauled in from wooded areas were too expensive for the farmer who could scarcely afford to pay the necessary filing fees for a claim and probably had to mortgage everything he owned to buy the basic equipment for farming. Even heating and cooking had to be performed with the heat of burning cobs, twisted grass, or buffalo chips and cow wood—as it was called by the more polite pioneers.

Imagine the despair of travelling 10,000 miles—or even 1,000 miles —to make a new start. At last the pioneer reached the selected land on the Nebraska plains. He had a wagon drawn by two horses, a few supplies, an axe, a plow, a shovel, a barrel or two, a canary, a wife, and three kids. With this he had to build a home. There was not a tree to be seen—in fact, none had been seen for three days. There were no rocks, no stone outcroppings. There was absolutely nothing but sky and grass.

The scene has all the makings of a twentieth century science-fiction story—a spaceship, stranded on a barren, desert planet with no available resources except the pilot's hands and mind. But no twentieth-century engineer could have solved the problem better. The sod house, as was eventually proved, was not only an adequate solution but also a comfortable one. It transcended the level of mere shelter and became a home; in some cases it was as comfortable and clean as the homes the pioneers left in the East—and it was constructed at a fraction of the cost.

A recent testimony of the comfort possible in a sod house is that of a man named Swisher, who built a soddy in July, 1932, three miles north of Halsey in Thomas County.

It is cheap, cool in summer, warm in winter. The sod house laughs at hard times and keeps alive old traditions. (State Historical Society Archives)

The earliest sod houses in Nebraska were those built by the Mormons at Winter Camp, north of the present site of Omaha. They may have borrowed the idea from the Omaha Indians, who, in this very area, lived in earth and timber lodges, or from English settlers in the Great Lakes area who built turf houses in the style of earth houses sometimes built for temporary shelter in Great Britain.

The restrictions on old, traditional materials and experiments with the new produced some interesting and unusual forms. Everett Dick in *The Sod-House Frontier* describes some of the grotesque attempts:

At Lawrence, Kansas, many odd structures were to be seen. There were dugouts, sod houses, log cabins, shake structures, and other odd dwelling places. In the summer of 1854 it was a village of tents, but by the following year most of the houses were made of sod. The sod house built at this time had not developed into the standard type which came into being on the plains in the next pioneer generation. Sod was used for the walls but not for the entire house as was done on the true sod-house frontier. A style which became fairly common and which was almost peculiar to Lawrence at this time was called "the hay tent." It was built by setting up two rows of poles and then bringing them together at the top and thatching the sides with prairie hay. The house was all roof and gable; the windows and doors were in the end. The gables were built with sod walls.

As the sod house developed it became clear that it could successfully meet the climatic and geographic limitations of the plains (discussed in detail on pages 122-28). Its thick walls and roof provided a perfect insulation against the intense heat of Nebraska summers and the cold of winters.

The snow lay on the ground a long time, and the winter was cold. We had no coal but the house, built almost half underground with walls three feet thick and a dirt roof fifteen to eighteen inches thick, didn't need much fuel. We had no radiators nor water pipes to thaw in those days. (Mrs. Hope Gates Swick, Pioneer Stories)

Some of the present generation think it must be very unpleasant to live in a sod house, but I'm telling you they are the most comfortable all-year around house I ever lived in; they are cool in summer and warm in winter and the elements don't bother you unless the roof leaks, which sometimes happens. (Herman Albert, Pioneer Stories)

The harsh winds that swept the plains were more damaging than they are now because there were no windbreaks, hedgerows, trees or buildings; the sod wall—especially when plastered—completely shuts out these winds. In the few incidents of Indian warfare, sod proved to be good fortress material, stopping arrows and slowing bullets. Tornados frequently tore away the roof—the soddy's weakest point—but even then the walls always remained standing and the families huddled inside were far safer than they would have been in frame houses that literally explode when hit by a tornado.

Some informants claimed that a weakness of the sod house was its susceptibility to fire, for the walls were in reality as much the woody stems and roots of grasses as soil and sand, and once the soil had dried, the woody parts became as flammable as tinder, but the evidence seems to contradict this. Not one of the more than four hundred pioneer accounts surveyed for this study document the burning of a sod house—even though one does mention the ignition of a cloth false-ceiling near a hot chimney. On the contrary, the frequent descriptions of prairie grass fires—perhaps the single most recurrent threat during early settlement—note that people fled to the sanctuary of the soddy, and that, while the roof grasses might burn and the room fill with smoke, the houses remained standing. Whenever a firebreak had been made by plowing and back-burning or when there was time for wetting the walls and roof thoroughly before the approach of the fire, the sod house proved to be a reliable refuge.

The sod house, since it was folk architecture, displayed great variation, the most common characteristic of any type of folklore. For example, a song like "Sweet Nebraska Land" was sung to many tunes, some quite similar, others very different; words and verses were changed from place to place, adapted often to fit local situations and circumstances. The titles varied from "Sweet Kansas Land" to "Sweet Saskatchewan." No one variant is the correct one; they are all equally valid, just as no one recipe for apple pie is the "correct" one.* This is also true of the styles and variations of the sod house. There was no one correct version, only more and less common forms. Each sod house represented a part of the spectrum of sod house construction and, indeed, the sod house was a range of types rather than one single form, with adaptations developed for variations of geography, climate, resources, and the skills of the builder.

*For further discussion of this song, its text and music, see Pages 180-183

Illustration 6

Nothing can better illustrate the wide variety in types and quality of sod houses than the above dugout near Roten Valley in Custer County, Nebraska, and the famous Gordon Haumont house twelve miles northeast of Broken Bow, Nebraska. While the dugout has no windows, a sod chimney, a three-plank door, and one beam, the Haumont house has a shingled roof, brick chimney, split door — and even one double window. (Nebraska State Historical Society)

Illustration 7

Perhaps the most fundamental variant of the examples used for this study is time. Butcher's pictures cover a period of almost ten years and, since many of the photos are of soddies that may already have been ten or twelve years old, the variation in age of the sod houses may be closer to twenty years. Personal descriptions of sod houses range from the mid-nineteenth century almost to the mid-twentieth: the latest soddy I have found was built in 1940 near Dunning, Nebraska, by J. Dean Hersh.

Illustration 8

Two views of what may be the last sod house to have been built within the Nebraska sod house tradition. The Hersh family built the house in 1940 near Dunning, Nebraska, Blaine County. (Courtesy of Dean Hersh)

Illustration 9

As time passed it became increasingly easy to obtain lumber, shingles, tar paper, plaster, paint, hardware, and concrete, and for this reason the later sod houses obviously show an increased refinement. Earlier settlers had less chance to find a home with neighbors while their own house was being erected, so their houses often reflect the haste with which they were built. Later immigrants were also more likely to be far more sophisticated about tools and techniques of sod construction than were the builders ten or twenty years before.

Individual houses, of course, varied in proportion to the skill, need, financial resources, and resolve of the builder himself. A bachelor who had little need of a luxurious, spacious house and who hoped soon to have a reason to build a finer house, can scarcely be condemned for not expending the energy to build a sod house like that in photograph 6. It is clear that a man with money could build a better house than a poor man, even where sod was the building material. The man who had previously built four soddies and had a grasshopper plow and a cutting spade produced a more polished product than the newly arrived Dane. The man who could live in a covered wagon with his wife for a month while he found a good site, selected the best sod, and carefully raised his walls was likely to have a finer finished product than the man who stepped off the train with a wife, four children, and a bag of carpenter tools.

The processes and features treated and described in this book result from the study and compilation of pioneer accounts, interviews, pictures, previous studies, and field examinations of extant soddies.*

*For a list of names and a bibliography see the appendix.

Of course, the conclusions are valid primarily for the Custer County sod houses, because most of the primary materials, pictures, and interviews are from Custer County, but those materials from other parts of Nebraska suggest quite clearly that the Custer County sod house was a representative example of the Nebraska sod house in general, embodying most of the common features while also displaying the breadth of variation.

The Site:

The prospective land claimant first sought land that seemed productive. He looked for rich, dark soil (although the yellow Nebraska loess also proved to be quite fertile), good water—evidenced by a creek or slough, timber and good grass. To facilitate tilling, he tried to secure a claim with a minimum of vertical acreage—canyons, draws, and hills. He tried to avoid drifting sand and blowouts that like a cancer could spread and ruin more of the claim. He hoped to settle near a community for the safety and convenience inherent in this proximity; when this was not possible, he sought out a good trail or railroad which could bring him closer to a town in terms of time if not in actual distance. Finally, he avoided wherever possible settling where an impassable river or canyon isolated him from civilization.

After filing and paying his fees the settler had to select the best location on his claim to build his sod house. A favorite spot was at the bottom of a shallow canyon wall. Nestled in such a hollow the house was protected from hot and cold winds, blowing snow and sand, and tornados. The canyon wall also protected the sod house from the summer sun, but this advantage turned into a disadvantage in the winter when the warm sun was more welcome.

Most Nebraska sod houses were to some degree "dugouts"; that is, the houses were dug back into a bank. This eliminated some of

Illustration 10

This dugout, belonging to the Burgert family, one mile south of Westerville and photographed by Butcher in 1887, had a fine example of the three-beam, lightly sodded roof. It is also one of the few Butcher pictures showing an outhouse. (Nebraska State Historical Society)

the work of erecting walls and provided a firmer wall. Locating at the base of a slope permitted the use of the valley wall as a back or side wall of the house.

A site in a draw also brought the house closer to the best building materials. The toughest and thickest grasses were slough grass, blue stem, and buffalo grass, found in such depressions, and the soil there tended to have a firmer clay cement than the sandier soils of the toplands. Furthermore, if there was ground moisture to be found, it would be in the valleys, closest to the water table, and all informants agreed that moist sod provided the firmest sod blocks. Finally, if there were trees and brush for the roof and furniture, they would be found in the canyons.

Big Blue Stem Grass was the king of the prairie grasses. It grew as high as a horse's shoulder and was so rich and lush that no weeds could grow where there was a strand of Big Blue Stem. If it was to be used for sod construction, the grass had to be mowed so that the sods would fit firmly together; the cut grass was then used for sheathing the roof.

BIG
BLUE
STEM

RLW

PRAIRIE CORDGRASS
ALSO CALLED
"SLOUGH GRASS" OR
MARSH GRASS

Slough Grass was almost as popular as Buffalo Grass. It grew a good deal higher than Buffalo Grass and therefore was often used for sheathing roofs. Slough Grass grew in moist draws and, as its name suggests, in sloughs.

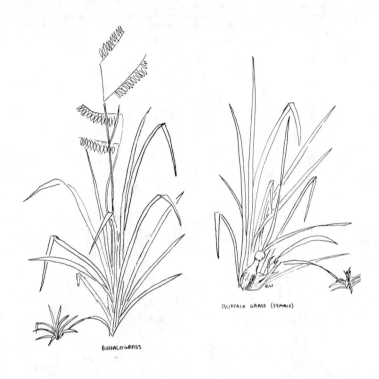

BUFFALO GRASS

BUFFALO GRASS (FEMALE)

One of the most popular sod grasses for house construction was Buffalo Grass. It was short and tough and in the fall its roots were wiry and woody. Buffalo Grass grew on the tops of hills and has both a male and female gender.

WIRE GRASS (PRAIRIE THREEAWN)

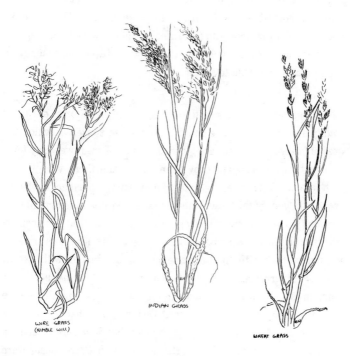

WIRE GRASS
(NIMBLE WILL)

INDIAN GRASS

WHEAT GRASS

Although Wheat Grass, Indian Grass. and Wire Grasses were not as common as **Buffalo Grass, Slough** Grass, or Big Blue Stem, there were many stands of them and **their roots** cemented the sods in many prairie homes.

The primary danger to be avoided in the lowlands was the flash flood, which meant that the most danger was in the best sites—in the valleys and canyons. Flooding could be avoided to some degree by building as high as possible on the slope and at a wide place where the water could spread out in a shallow sheet. While this consideration could not be ignored, the danger was not so great that it overcame the desire to build in the canyons, out of the wind.

Preparation of the Site:

Although the best building time was in the fall when the native prairie grasses had become woody and acquired tough, wire-like roots, the homesteader seldom could choose his time. He had to decide first what the floor plan and size of his house were to be, depending on the size of his family and the amount of work and money he was prepared and able to spend.

Most sod houses were simple rectangles. *Pioneer Stories of Custer County* furnishes over one hundred sod-house stories in which the sizes of twelve sod houses are given. Three measured twelve by fourteen feet, two were sixteen by twenty-four, and there were one of each measuring fourteen by sixteen, fourteen by fourteen, twelve by twelve, sixteen by thirty-two, nine by nine (too small incidentally for pre-emption requirements), twelve by twenty-four and fourteen by twenty-four. Measurements of fourteen feet, with nine occurrences, and twelve feet, with eight occurrences, predominated, with sixteen feet (six occurrences) and twenty-four feet (four occurrences) less common but not rare. Interviews and letters suggest that these were indeed common proportions. Everett Dick remarks that, . . . *a rather pretentious sod house followed a common building plan of sixteen feet wide and twenty feet long.* He also notes that sod houses were frequently faced to the South; the walls were aligned with the North Star on a clear night.

Although the rectangular floor plan was most common—because of the simplicity of its layout—there were also L-floor, or dog-leg, soddies (see illustrations 11 and 41) and T-floor plans (illustration 12); often the "legs" of these plans were later additions, built on to accommodate an expanding family or economy. The addition of a room away from a hillside eliminated the need for digging and leveling as was necessary when the addition followed the original lay of the floor plan. The L-floor and T-floor also provided pleasant corners protected from the incessant winds, where clothes could be spread on the grass to dry, where children could play, or where the adults might gather for a game of croquet. In the Butcher collection are fifty-seven L-floor houses and three T-floors.

L-floor plan soddy

Illustration 11

L-floor plans like the one of this sod house were very popular, for they provided a quiet corner out of the wind. The Mat Freeman house, located near West Old Jefferson in Custer County, had a board sheathed roof with three plank beams. Solomon D. Butcher's wagon stands at the left. (Nebraska State Historical Society)

Illustration 12

A T-floor house. Swene Pike, Jefferson, Nebraska, 1886. (Nebraska State Historical Society)

The T-floor plan.

A very rare form was the round house. In the last half of the nineteenth century the round and multi-sided house (especially the octagonal house) enjoyed great popularity in America. In Nebraska, especially in the eastern part of the state, there are still several polyhedral houses standing. (There are two directly south of Nebraska City, for example.) Even Butcher's collection contains some photographs of multi-sided houses. Approximately thirty-five round and polyhedral barns were built in Nebraska before the First World

War. And of course the Omaha Indian earth lodge, possibly the great-grandfather of the Nebraska sod house, was round. The Butcher collection includes one round sod house from Cherry County, which can be seen in illustration 13.

Illustration 13

This round soddy was in Cherry County on Gordon Creek. It is uncertain whether this photograph was actually taken by Butcher. (Nebraska State Historical Society)

If there were to be internal dividing walls, it was best that they too be planned at this time, for if they were added very long after the original construction, disparate settling caused cracking and buckling of the walls and ceilings.

Once a size and floor plan had been decided on, stakes were set and the digging begun. On level ground the builder might immediately begin laying sod, without even bothering to clear off the sod on the site of the house, but usually the ground was cleared of grass and carefully leveled with a sharp spade; the sod was saved to be used in filling cracks and holes. Snake and gopher holes in the foundation and floor area were filled with loose dirt and tamped solid. Sometimes the entire floor area was wetted and tamped with a fence post into a concrete-hard base.

Only occasionally did a sod craftsman prepare footings for the walls by driving posts into the ground, by actually pouring concrete footings, or by laying brick or stone bases (especially under the corners where the walls were heaviest) in the rare locales where good clay or stone could be found—and afforded.

Cutting the Sod:

Occasionally, before cutting the sod with the plow, a cutter or disc was run across the sod to pre-cut it into convenient blocks.

To start with a sod cutter was used. It was similar to a corn planter except the knives were just straight iron bars sharpened on the front side instead of the wide shoes used on a planter. Two or three men rode on the cutter to force the knives into the sod the depth that you wished to plow—preferably four inches. The sod was cut crosswise of the way the plowing was to be done; this saved having to cut the sod into smaller pieces with a spade . . . . If the grass was too high it might have to be mowed, as too much grass would be hard to handle and the sod would not pack so tight and the settling would be very uneven. Four-inch grass or shorter was best. (David Simms, Mason City)

The single most important tool for sod-house construction was the "proper" plow. The common "turning" plow, that digs deep and tumbles the furrow could not be used, for it destroys the sod. The ideal tool was the "cutting" or grasshopper plow. In place of the turning plow's mould board, a sheet of iron that tumbled the soil, the cutting plow had a set of adjustable rods that allowed the sod to be carefully cut into a long ribbon about three to six inches thick and one to one and one-half feet wide. As the cutting plow sliced through the virgin sod, the tearing grass roots made a sound like the opening of a gigantic zipper.

If the new settler did not have a cutting plow—and at first only a few did—a neighbor could be hired to cut sod. Often he was repaid in labor, perhaps during the next harvest season. Or he could meet the plow problem in the way Randall Sargent did, as told by Irene Dewey in *Pioneer Stories*.

. . . The first thing necessary was a plow with which to break the sod for their "soddy" and the fields of corn. Since Randall had no plow, he proceeded to make one from a small waterelm trunk. He hewed out a beam about four inches in diameter and four feet long. With his brother Riley's assistance he made a rod plow [cutting plow] patterned after a little plow called "The Antelope," which they had had in Iowa. The next spring he and his brother made a hundred of these plows and for a time were hardly able to supply the demand for them.

Illustration 14

Cutting plow: the flat blade shoved the sod from the prairie and the rods let it gently and unbroken to the ground.

Often horses were used to pull the plow, of course, for they were the most common work animals, but oxen were preferred for sod cutting because they pulled a good deal slower than horses. With this deliberate pace the sodbuster could take greater care in maintaining an even, continuous strip of sod.

The sods were cut to a size that could easily be handled by the workers—usually about three to four inches thick, one to one and one-half feet wide, and two to three feet long; the actual size depended on the thickness of the sod, the strength of the lifter, and the moisture content of the soil. The thicker and more moist the sod, the smaller the size.

Because of the importance of the moisture content, which insured a solid, easily handled and laid block, only enough sod was cut each morning to last for that day's work; sod was never left turned in the field if it was to be used in house construction, for the prairie winds would quickly dry it. In all it took a total of about one acre of sod for a standard twelve by fourteen-foot house.

A wagon was prepared for sod hauling by clearing off the bed and seats and laying heavy planks on its frame. Or a sod-boat or sledge was made—a set of wooden runners affixed to a wooden raft or forked tree trunk. It was preferable to have a low-built vehicle so that the workers would not have to lift the heavy sods any higher than absolutely necessary. Horses or oxen then hauled the sods to the building site.

If a period of bad weather slowed sod cutting, the man of the family would walk or drive to a store or village to purchase nails and lumber for door and window frames, fence posts for rafters, or tar paper and shingles for roofing. Poor homesteaders—that is, *most* homesteaders—went to the cedar canyons, especially the one about three and one-half miles northwest of Victoria Springs (although similar cedar groves were scattered along the valley walls of most Nebraska rivers and creeks) to select the longest, straightest possible cedar beams. The trip, the cutting, and the dressing of the timber took from three to five days.

Mother and children meanwhile combed the hillsides around the site of the future sod house for plum, chokecherry and willow brush for furniture construction and roof poles; and slough grass, buffalo grass, and wire grass, tough, woody grasses for sheathing the sod roof.

Laying the Walls:

The wagon load of "Nebraska marble," as wags often called it, was hauled from the low grounds, where the best wild grasses were to be found, to the house site. The laying began in a corner and then out the length of the wall. Each layer was finished before the next was begun; the layers were kept level. The sod bricks were laid virtually always with the grass side down; only one informant said "grass up." The bricks were always laid like bricks, and usually the walls were two or three sods thick, with these vertical layers also staggered. Thus no two vertical joints ever butted one against the other, and the winds, bugs, and snakes had to work harder to find a way in. Corners and wall bases were sometimes re-enforced with yet another course of sod.

Most accounts describe the use of a binding course. Every third or fourth layer of sod was laid crosswise to hold the inner and outer layers firmly together. Butcher's photographs also show that boards were occasionally used for the same purpose; see illustration 40.

The sods were laid in two or three rows and the seams between them were always staggered to keep the walls as tight as possible against winds, bugs, and rodents. As sods were piled atop the first layer, they too were staggered like bricks; this eliminated any one naturally weak seam where the walls might split. Every third or fourth layer was laid crosswise to bind the two stacks together.

Although no mortar was used to bind the sods together, all cracks between the bricks and any holes in them were carefully filled with loose soil. This made a more solid wall and closed possible entries to pests.

Great care had to be taken to keep the center line of the wall perfectly vertical. Because of the great weight of the walls, any lean at all caused the wall to settle unevenly and eventually to collapse. Though many sod houses were built with a very definite slant to the outside surface—to strengthen the bottom of the wall where washing and weight did their severest damage—the inside profile and center line of the wall were kept close to absolute vertical. (See illustration 15 for an example of the sloped wall.)

Sometimes before the third layer had been laid, the door frame was set and propped in place with a pole. The walls were built up around the frame. Similarly, as the desired level of the window sills was reached, the window frames were set into place. These frames were usually simple, open boxes made of pieces of one-inch lumber nailed together. One-inch holes were drilled through the lumber so that wooden rods that held the frame firmly in place in the wall could later be driven through the frame and into the surrounding sod.

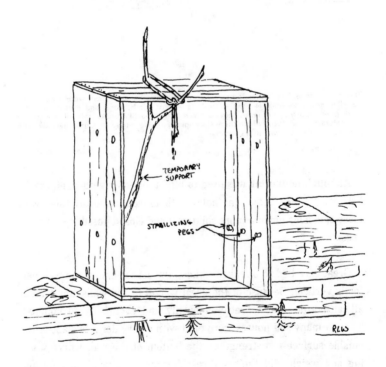

When the walls reached the level desired for the window sills — usually about two or three feet — the frames were set on the walls and propped in place with a stick. The walls were built up around the frames and later dowels or pegs were driven through one-inch holes in the frame into the walls to keep the windows firmly in place.

Illustration 15

This picture of the J. C. Cram house in Loup County, taken in 1886, is one of the most interesting of the Butcher collection. The five-beam roof construction and plank sheathing can be seen very easily. The slope of the outside walls, a feature seen in twenty-seven Butcher photographs, is very clear. Like many other sod houses in Nebraska the Cram house had a set of double windows, pet birds, a pile of elk horns, many house plants in windows, and a wooden fence. (Nebraska State Historical Society)

As the wall rose above waist level the wagon was driven along the wall and used as a platform to work from. While the man hoisted the heavy sods, his wife carefully shaved the walls, inside and out, with a sharp spade. This kept the walls balanced, helped the layer maintain a vertical profile, made the house look more finished, and helped close bug and rodent holes. The inside walls had to be shaved so that they could later be plastered.

When the level of the walls reached the tops of door and window frames, planks or boards (usually two) or cedar posts (usually three) were laid along the top of the wall and across the frames. These pieces supported the weight of the sod over the windows and prevented warping of the frames, which could jam the window or break the precious glass panes.

Frames were put in as the house was built. Six to eight inches were left above the doors and windows [that is, above the frames] for the house to settle. [In this space] they stuffed paper. (William Skelton, Broken Bow)

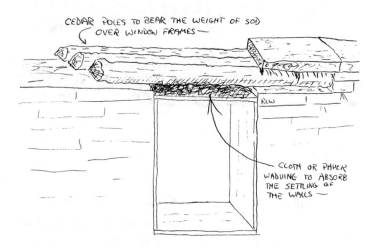

CEDAR POLES TO BEAR THE WEIGHT OF SOD OVER WINDOW FRAMES —

CLOTH OR PAPER WADDING TO ABSORB THE SETTLING OF THE WALLS —

To keep the weight of the walls and roof off of the window casements, cedar posts or planks were often laid above them. Since the walls under the window were lighter than the parts of the wall around them they did not settle as deeply. To even the settling—and avoid the jamming and breaking of the windows—a space filled with cloth or paper was left between the window casement and the over-beams.

When the walls were completed, re-enforcement was frequently added to the base of the walls, as mentioned above. Three or four planks might be set up along the foot of the wall, another layer of sod might be added to the outside wall, or even a short retaining wall of concrete might be poured to discourage erosion by dripping eave-water and digging by mice.

Roofing the Soddy:

Illustration   16

Frank Roach of Keith County, Nebraska, is pictured here (about 1890) as he was roofing a new addition to his soddy. He is using one main beam — the ridge pole — and five rafters. The man standing on the gable peak is about to close in the sod around the ridge pole. Then planks will be laid horizontally and covered with a light cover of sod, as has been done on the other part of the house. Note that the original section has also been neatly plastered. (Nebraska State Historical Society)

The roof was the most important element of the sod house. If the roof failed, the house failed, for the endurance of the walls depended ultimately on the protection of the roof. And there could be little cheer about the efficiency of the walls if the ceiling leaked snow and wind.

From hardly any rain we soon had more than we needed. Our roof would not stand the heavy downpours that sometimes continued for days at a time, and it would leak from one end to the other. We could keep our beds comparatively dry by drawing them into the middle of the room directly under the peak of the roof. Sometimes the water would drip on the stove while I was cooking, and I would have to keep tight lids on the skillets to prevent the mud from falling into the food. With my dress pinned up, and rubbers on my feet, I waded around until the clouds rolled by. Then we would clean house. Almost everything had to be moved outdoors to dry in the sun. Life is too short to be spent under a sod roof. (Mrs. H. C. Stuckey, in History of Custer County)

The faults of the sod roof were many. Its enormous weight demanded substantial wooden support, but since sod roofs were used because of the scarcity of wood for shingles, a satisfactory balance of wooden support was seldom approached. Any skimping led to the ultimate collapse of tons of soggy sod onto the meal table or bed.

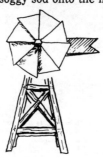

The disaster pictured here was multiplied a thousand times on the Nebraska plains. George Barns homesteaded near Clear Creek in Custer County; during the hard winter, his wife died and left him with three small children. His troubles were compounded even further when the roof of his sod house collapsed and smashed the bed to splinters—only moments after he and the children had left it The man in this picture had not only the every-day worries of weather and crops; he also had to find a home for the children and build a new one for himself. (Nebraska State Historical Society)

Sod—especially that of the sandy western Nebraska uplands—is very permeable; it leaks. Thickness of the roof made little difference, and not only did it leak when it rained, but the soaked sod continued to drip for another two or three days after it was sunny and dry outside.

This was partially because of the shallow pitches used on most sod house roofs. To avoid getting the gable end walls too high— an encouragement for eventual collapse—the roofs were kept shallow. Of course, if the roofs were made too steep, the sod slipped off. And the steeper the roof, the longer the rafters had to be—and once more the settler came up against the scarcity of timber, the source of so many of his problems. In short, steep roofs demanded more and longer pieces of wood, weakened end walls, and were likely on some stormy day to slip off into a muddy heap, exposing the household to the open sky; shallow roofs, on the other hand, leaked. Most families chose the leaky shallow pitch.

During the last years we lived in [our sod house, it] got pretty leaky. We were so glad for the good rains that caused us to have to get up and put dishpans, washpans, tubs, and skillets under the drips, that we did not mind. My dad used to say those drips played a regular tune with soprano, alto, tenor, and bass, in the harmony. (Mrs Leota Runyan)

And those who saved money on the roof and enjoyed instead the luxury of a plank floor wished they hadn't.

In the Spring when we had the big rains our roof did its share of leaking and even after the rain was over it seemed like our roof leaked for another day. Mother often wished that it was reversed— the boards on the roof instead of on the floor. (Mrs. Marie Gebhart Varney, Pioneer Stories)

Sod roofs, like sod walls, however, had advantages as well as disadvantages. They were cheap; some families could afford shingles, but not many—and even some shingled roofs were given a finishing touch of a layer of sod (see illustration 28). A sod roof was nominally fireproof, as mentioned above. It could, with some investment of

Illustration 18

Although this picture shows many interesting pioneer artifacts — a well digger with his scaffold, a dugout with a frame section around its lone window, a sod chimney, and a sheathed roof without its sod covering — the photo was chosen especially to show how gable ends and interior walls looked before the beams were set in place and the roof was laid (in upper right). (Jacob Graff farm, West Union, Nebraska. Photographed in 1887. Nebraska State Historical Society)

money, time, and effort, be a sound, waterproof roof, and during the spring and summer it was very attractive: flowers bloomed all along the eaves, meadowlarks—feeling quite at home—sang on the ridge, and the green grass of the roof blended pleasantly with the surrounding grassy hills. Its insulating qualities were superb. It moderated the summer heat and kept the soddy surprisingly warm in the winter—a quality that was paramount on the Nebraska plains, where the scarcity of fuel was no less intense than the scarcity of building materials. That dirt and sod could be used for an efficient roof had already be amply proven by the sod roofs so common throughout Scandinavia and, closer to home, by the Indian earth lodges in eastern Nebraska.

Lifting the heavy cedar beams into their notches in the gable ends was a problem—especially when there were only two or three men to do the work. Usually, the builders set two poles against the eave wall and with ropes rolled the beams up onto their positions.

Roof Types:

There were primarily three designs of roofs used on the Nebraska sod house: the gable roof, the hipped roof, and the shed, or lean-to, roof.

Gable roof:

The most common style of sod house roof was the gable roof. This style can be seen, for example, in illustrations 19, 20, 21, and 22. If this form was to be used, the end walls of the house were built up from both side walls to form the pyramid-shaped end wall. Before the wall had reached a peak, poles were leaned against the soddy walls, and the ridge pole was rolled up the poles into a prepared notch at the top of the gable wall. The sod was then built up around the pole.

This ridge pole and the other two, four, or six beams were usually cedar because, despite the difficulty of finding a long straight beam, cedar was a tough, rot-resistant wood. This was important to the sod house builder, for the beams were covered later with sod and were therefore subject to moisture, insects, bacteria, and extreme stress. Wherever a long span was used, a support was propped up in the middle of the house, running from the floor to the beam. This same device was used to permit the use of two shorter beams, butted end-to-end over the support. A beam that by good fortune extended beyond the end wall of the house was seldom cut off, for it provided a convenient place to hang game for cleaning and food to dry.

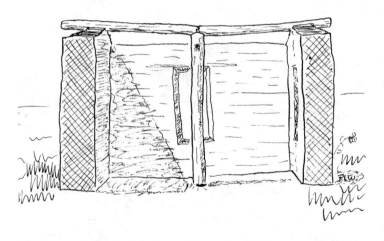

Whenever two short beams had to be used for a ridge pole they were supported in the center of the house by an upright post set into the ground. Even when one solid beam had to bear a very heavy roof, a post might be set in the center to offer additional support and take some of the strain from the end walls.

The ridge pole, especially if it was the only roof beam, had a decided tendency to push down into the sod of the end wall. To ease

this stress, forked posts were frequently set under the ridge pole—
sometimes inside, sometimes outside. Inside, the pole was a convenient and sturdy place to hang coats and lanterns, but outside, it took
up less of the precious interior space of the soddy.

The ridge pole — usually a cedar beam — had to bear all of the weight of the massive
roof. Because of the weight on it it sometimes started to push down through the gable
walls. To remedy this, upright beams were set into the ground at either end of the house.
Most houses had the end uprights inside where they could be used to hang things on
—pots, clothes, and photographs, for example—but some, like this one, put the post outside to save room inside.

Of the photographs of Custer County sod houses in the Butcher
collection, the number of beams could be counted in a total of two
hundred and fourteen houses; fifty-one had only one beam, one
hundred three had three beams, fifty-five had five beams, and five
had seven. The others showed peculiar or variant numbers or the

beams could not be seen in the photographs. The more beams the builder used, the fewer and lighter rafters and sheathing, poles and planks were needed. When logs or rough-hewn beams were not used, single or double pieces of cut lumber (usually one-by-sixes or eights) were used; see illustrations 19 and 20, for example.

Illustration 19

This house near the Triumph post office in Custer County, Nebraska, was an excellent example of the one-beam house. Planks were run from the tops of the walls to the main ridge pole beam and a light board was nailed across the bottom of the eaves to keep the sod from sliding off. Although the house is small, the single window shows some wealth, for window panes of such size were very expensive. (Photographed in 1892. Nebraska State Historical Society)

Illustration 20

The fine sod home with its three-beam, heavily sodded roof (note that it has two layers of sod) will soon be abandoned for the new frame house on the hill. The well has a winch frame made of poles; an oaken bucket sits on the curbing. Note the children's wagon standing before the well. (Custer County. Photographed in 1887. Nebraska State Historical Society)

Illustration 21

The roof of the A. H. Pernie house near Lone Tree, Nebraska, was pegged around the edges to keep the sod from sliding. Note also the children's wagon and the drilled well with its fragile, pole winch-frame to the right. (Photographed in 1887. Nebraska State Historical Society)

Illustration 22

The Hartley Ranch house on the Middle Loup River sported a pole-and-brush porch. The ever-present elk horns lie on the roof and two bird cages grace the eaves of the house. Note that the ridge pole is supported by an external post. This picture, taken in 1886, is one of the few to show a pump in the farm yard. (Nebraska State Historical Society)

The most obvious advantages of the gable roof were the simplicity of its frame construction and the short lengths needed for rafters and sheathing. Its primary disadvantages were, as mentioned above, the increased height of the end walls and the length of the ridge pole.

Five hundred and sixty-four houses in the Butcher collection had gable roofs.

Hipped roof:

The hipped roof accounted for nineteen per cent of the seven hundred and thirty-six photographs of Custer County sod houses in the Butcher collection; for examples of this type of roof, see illustrations 23, 25, and 40. Its complexity of framing was compensated for by the even plate level (top surface of the walls) and the shorter lengths needed for the ridge pole (which was in turn offset by the need for two internal ridge pole supports). The two vertical supports held up one main beam and then from each corner of the house walls were extended four corner poles or rafters to the ends of the ridge pole. Willow rods were laid crosswise on these before the sheathing and cover were laid. In some areas of Nebraska the hipped roof is still referred to as a "sod-house roof."

Illustration 23
Many Butcher photographs include melons or squash to show one of the wealths of the new Nebraska lands. This house, near Dale, had a large, lumber porch, and on the new house in the background can be seen the framing for a hipped roof. (Photographed in 1888. Nebraska State Historical Society)

Illustration **24**

Although the outer covering of plaster had begun to wash off the W. H. Blair house near Broken Bow, the hipped roof, with its sod flashing on the ridges, was still in good condition when this picture was taken in 1888. To complete the elegance of the family portrait, the sewing machine has been brought to the foreground. (Nebraska State Historical Society)

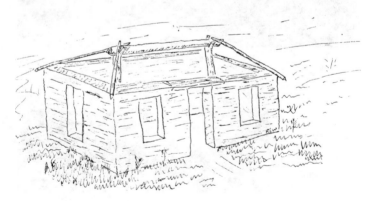

The hipped roof usually used two uprights inside the house with one major cross beam. Then, from each corner of the house, lighter poles were leaned against the main, ridge pole.

60

One of the disadvantages of the hipped roof was the difficulty presented when the homesteader wanted to add to the house. A gable-roof house could always be extended out one gable end but the absence of the gable end on the hipped roof made adding a room a more difficult undertaking. A lean-to however could be added, and often was, to an eave side and the roof was then simply continued down over the addition; for an example, see illustration 25.

Illustration 25

Although many, many sod houses were covered with plaster or cement in later years, the Morrison Gandy house near Broken Bow was completely plastered when photographed in 1886. It was difficult to add to a house with a hipped roof, but here two lean-tos have been added to the end eaves. A convenient cellar runs beneath the addition on the right of the photograph. (Nebraska State Historical Society)

The reduction of attic area under a hipped roof was on one hand an advantage since it cut down on the area to be heated above the floor and was a disadvantage on the other hand in that it cut down on precious storage area under the rafters.

The pyramid roof was a close relative of the hipped roof, but instead of the corner poles running to a central ridge pole they ran to a single pole set in the middle of the house. This kind of roof could only be used on a small houses. Because of the bank on the right side of the picture the builder of this soddy could not stand his window upright, so he just put it on its side so that it could be slid open.

A small house offered the possibility of a variation of the hipped roof, the pyramid roof. For this style, the length of the ridge pole was simply reduced to one point. A heavy vertical pole was set in the middle of the house and from each corner a pole was set into the crotch of this post. A disadvantage of the pyramid was the requirement of four long poles to serve as rafters running from each corner. Obviously, this more than balanced the advantage of the elimination of the ridge pole. Only four pyramid roofs occur in the photographs taken by Butcher.

Illustration 26
This southwest Custer County soddy is the best example of the Pyramid roof in the Butcher collection. (Photographed in 1892. Nebraska State Historical Society)

Lean-to roof.

Another rare form—and with good reason—was the lean-to or shed roof. Its advantages were few: if the short wall was set to the north, less wall area was exposed to cold winds and this not only kept the house warm but also reduced the pressures exerted against

Not many Nebraska sod houses had lean-to roofs like this, but a few—especially those that were built to last only a short time—did take advantage of its ease of construction.

the house by the wind; in this regard the lean-to roof is like a small version of the salt-box house discussed below. In the case of a small house, the lean-to roof was the simplest possible structure.

Its disadvantages were many: it required long rafters for the amount of area covered; it was easily blown off by a wind from the high-wall side; to allow for head room the walls had to be high and were therefore often unstable; and the tendency of the roof to slip down-slope often buckled and collapsed the walls.

Illustration 27

This rare shed-roof soddy stood on the Annie Walker homestead near Mason City, Nebraska. (Photo courtesy Leota Runyan)

Usually this type of roof was used only on small sheds, shacks, or animal shelters. The back wall was then only three or four feet high while the front was six to eight feet high. This was a quick and functional structure. A plank, log, or pole was laid along the top of both the front and back walls, poles were laid across these, and the roof was then covered with the conventional layer of sod.

Roof Frames of Lumber:

A much better roof could be made with two-by-four rafters joined carefully, usually with nails, to the ridge pole (usually a pair of one-by-sixes), spread across two or four one-by-six beams, and spaced evenly along the roof every two or three feet. This framework was then sheathed with one-inch planks. If the planks were placed vertically from the ridge pole to the eaves, strips of lath were frequently laid along the joints to prevent or reduce the leaking of water and soil. Horizontally laid sheathing, that is, running from gable to gable, was sometimes lapped, also to prevent leakage, or, if it could be afforded, lap-joint or rabbeted lumber would be purchased for use as roof sheathing.

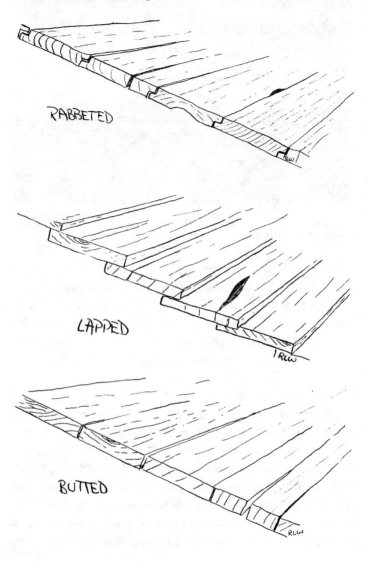

RABBETED

LAPPED

BUTTED

When the plank sheathing was laid vertically, that is, from the ridge pole to the walls, and no tarpaper was to be used, strips of lath were laid along the joints to discourage leaking.

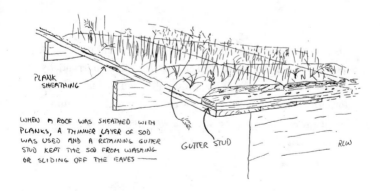

PLANK SHEATHING

WHEN A ROOF WAS SHEATHED WITH PLANKS, A THINNER LAYER OF SOD WAS USED AND A RETAINING GUTTER STUD KEPT THE SOD FROM WASHING OR SLIDING OFF THE EAVES ——

GUTTER STUD

RLW

The most important structural feature of this kind of polished, two-by-four frame, sheathed roof construction was the rafter chord. Not only were the rafters joined together with nails at the roof peak, but there were also two-by-four rafters (called chords) running from eave to eave (actually, from plate to plate). The roof frame profile was then a triangle, the strongest structural brace. When this construction was used, the weight of the roof no longer pushed outward, as it did with other types of roofs; now the roof was one solid unit and the weight was pushing straight down onto the broad shoulders of the sod walls.

Frameless sheathing:

A cheaper and substantially less efficient variation of this construction simply called for planks running vertically from the wall top (plate) to the ridge pole, over perhaps a beam or two but with no vertical rafters. As described above, strips of lath were often laid lengthwise over the joints to discourage leaking. The problem with this type of roofing was the tendency of the planks to warp and eventually break under the weight and moisture of the overlying sod.

Over the sheathing planks, the sod could be laid directly, or tarpaper or canvas could be tacked on first, then overlaid by sod. Shingles were occasionally used instead of sod, if the builder could afford them and if a freight line could bring them within reach. When canvas, tar paper, or shingles were used in conjunction with sod, the result was a firm, tight, and very efficient roof.

Even when shingles were used, sod was occasionally laid over them for insulation. Although shingles had the obvious advantages

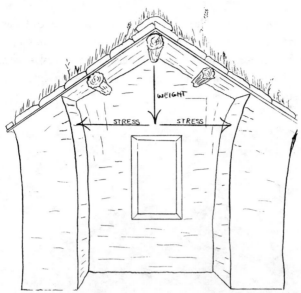

One of the principal weaknesses of the sod roof was the frequent omission of a 'chord' raf-ter. without these horizontal rafters the weight of the roof was transformed into stresses pushing out on the walls, and the resilient sod walls gave way to the stress. When chords were used however the weight exerted a vertical stress, which the heavy walls could easily bear.

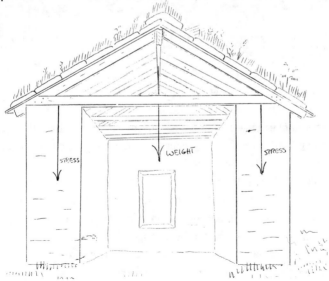

of keeping the house drier and more handsome, the cost was prohibitive and, when they were used without an overlay of sod, the resulting lightness caused as much trouble as the excessive weight of the sod roof, for the lighter shingle roof was easily lifted off in a windstorm.

Illustration 28

Even when shingles were used on a sod house, a covering of sod was frequently added because of its superlative insulating quality. (W. H. Burdett farm, southwest Custer County. Photographed in 1892. Nebraska State Historical Society)

Brush and pole roofing:

Although a majority of the Butcher sod houses were sheathed with lumber (five hundred one out of seven hundred thirty-six), many, especially the early houses, used a pole and brush construction for roof framing. Over cedar beams were laid vertically willow poles eighteen to twenty-four inches apart, running from the ridge pole to wall top. Atop these was piled a layer of green plum or chokecherry brush, and then atop this a layer of domestic hay or, even better, wild grasses. Some roofs added at this point a layer of fine yellow clay that could be found about eight to twelve feet below the ground surface or along arroyo walls, or a thin coating of plaster-like mud from the white beds of dry alkali lakes. This layer provided a virtually impermeable shield against moisture.

Sod was then put on the roof. It could be one to three layers thick, lapped or butted, thick or thin, depending on the desire of the builder and the strength of the underpinnings. If the roof was to be left as bare sod, the sod was laid grass side up so that it would continue to grow, to re-establish roots, to form a protective layer of grass and to prevent erosion; if the roof was to be plastered, the sod was laid grass side down, for this then presented a smooth, firm surface for the cement, which was made of the same clay or alkali mud mentioned above, mixed with some fine sand or ashes.

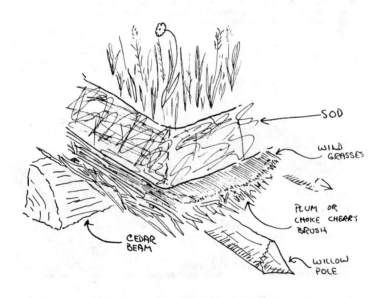

The typical sod roof rested on cedar beams and willow-pole rafters. Atop the poles was laid a layer of wild plum or chokecherry brush, then wild grass, occasionally then a layer of fine clay or gypsum, and finally the sod — grass up.

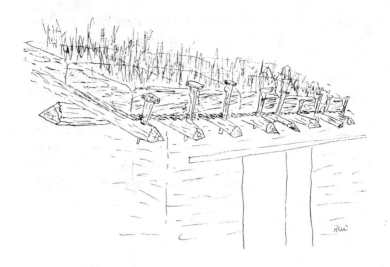

To keep the sod from sliding off of the roof sod house builders sometimes inserted wooden pegs or pins in the end of the rafters. Poles were also driven down through the rafters or beams into the walls to help keep the roof from blowing away.

Illustration   29

The windows of this house are very unusual because only a few sod houses used recessed windows; it was much more efficient to have them set at the outside edge of the casement. Note also the pole roof with no cut lumber. This picture was taken around 1886 in East Custer County. (Nebraska State Historical Society)

BUTTED SOD
ROOF

RLW

Sod could be laid on the roof in two styles: butted or lapped. The butted technique called for the sods to be placed end by end and side by side — tightly to prevent leaks. The idea of overlapping the sods was to prevent leaks, to approach a shingle-like roof. Unfortunately the little valleys formed by the lapping provided convenient spots for the water to stop and seep through.

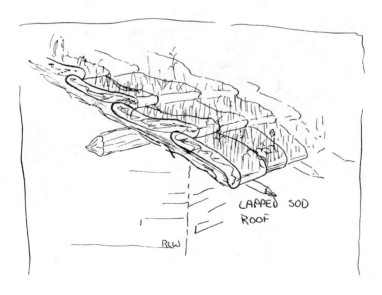

LAPPED SOD
ROOF

RLW

Illustration 30

The roof of this house is a fine example of the sod-on-grass-on-poles-on-beams construction. Pegs have been driven into the ends of the pole rafters to prevent sod from slipping off of the roof. The front wall has been plastered with a clay-and-sand mortar. Photographed in 1890. Nebraska State Historical Society)

Illustration 31

Although this photograph of the John U. Kleeb house near Round Valley was chosen to illustrate a lapped-sod roof, it also shows many of the most common characteristics of the Nebraska sod house: windows flush with the outer wall, prominent windmill, elk horns, narrow eaves, a child's wagon, and a bird cage. The planks around the windows are unique and were probably used to make the frames tighter. This Butcher photograph was made in 1886. (Nebraska State Historical Society)

Illustration 32

Solomon Butcher took this picture of the Reeder soddy near Merna, Nebraska, in 1886. The gable roof has butted-sod covering with no eaves to catch the prairie winds. The twelve-pane sash- windows have slightly bevelled window wells and potted plants sit both in the windows and on the outside the house. (Nebraska State Historical Society)

One consideration that was important and that presented yet another dilemma in roof construction was the width of the eaves. On one hand, wide eaves would have protected the vulnerable walls from rain erosion; on the other, wide eaves caught the prairie wind like a kite, and once in a while a good gale would flip a sod house roof off the walls and into some canyon, where the sod-house family would have to salvage whatever lumber and beams they could and go about the process of reroofing the house from scratch. The likelihood of this was increased by the fact that there was no way to anchor the roof firmly to the loose sod walls. Only its massive weight held it on, for few homesteaders could afford to buy iron rods to sink down into the walls for use as roof anchors. A few builders solved the problem by guying the roof to the ground with wires or ropes; others drove wooden stakes down through the roof and into the sod walls.

Three or four sod houses shown in the Butcher collection were built with thatched roofs, usually with a thatch of prairie grass. The unusual round house (illustration 13), for example, had a thatched roof, which was then covered with sod. Several pictures in the collection show barns with thatched roofs.

Illustration 33

The barn on this homestead in southwest Custer County sports a thatched roof. Such roofs were usually made of domestic hay or wild grass — especially big bluestem. The roof of the house is shingled. Many prairie farm families, like this one, carefully nursed a spindly sapling brought to the farmyard from nearby river bottoms. (Photographed in 1892. Nebraska State Historical Society)

Illustration 34

This view of the McCoslin farmstead near Rose Valley, Nebraska, shows a massive barn with a crude straw roof and a soddy without a roof (to the left). (Photographed in 1886.. Nebraska State Historical Society)

Windows and doors:

The most common type of window was the twelve-pane double-frame sash window that permitted lowering the top or lifting the bottom frames for ventilation. The sod walls did not permit the use of counterweights, so the windows were simply propped open with sticks (see illustration 77). The short walls of a few houses, especially dugouts, discouraged the use of the tall double frames and the twelve-panes were then set horizontally in the walls. This provided the same amount of window area and allowed opening and closing by sliding the frame horizontally. (See illustration 38 for this kind of window.)

A few houses used six-pane windows (half sections). These were either permanently fixed in place or they swiveled horizontally on pins set in the side frames. (For this type window, see illustration 37.)

In small spaces where larger twelve-pane windows would not fit or when there was not enough money to buy twelve-panes, half-frames with six window panes were used. Of course this single unit could not slide open like the double-frame twelve-pane, but it was often mounted on pins in the frame so that it could be swung open to provide ventilation.

Windows were usually as large and numerous as possible, however, for the insides of soddies had a tendency to be dark: deep window and door wells diminished any light coming in at an angle, dark walls (if not plastered) and ceilings (if not covered) reflected little light, and artificial lighting was rare and at best inadequate.

Most sod houses had windows on all sides except where the ground level was so high on one or two sides that there was no room for windows between the eaves and the ground. Most windows were set out in their wells toward the edge of the outer walls (see illustration 32) rather than flush with the inside wall (see illustration 37). This meant that any bevelling of the window casement was inside rather than outside, leaving the sill space inside for potted plants, shelves and window seats rather than outside where water could settle and wash. The deep window wells found unusual use during heavy rains: a homesteading family often had to sit in the frames because everywhere else in the house water poured through the ceiling. Today, sod houses that have been plastered, stuccoed or sheathed with clapboards can still be recognized by their deep-set windows. The bevelling permitted light to enter at a much broader angle.

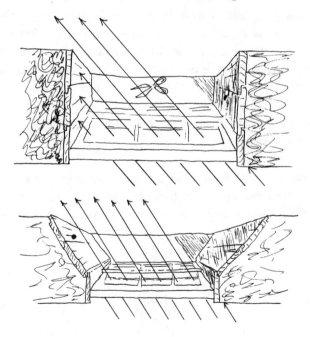

To increase window area and yet avoid small columns of sod between casements—columns that might easily collapse and could support no weight—many soddies (forty from the Butcher collection) had double and even triple windows, that is, multiple frames set side by side. For examples of double windows see illustrations 35 and 15; a triple frame occurs in illustration 36. These multiple frames must have provided a good deal of light, for they also eliminated the light loss that resulted when the windows were separated and encased on all sides within the heavy sod walls.

In another effort to bring light into the house many builders plastered the insides of the window frames thus preventing the deep, dark shadows made by bare sod.

When panes broke, they could not always be immediately replaced. Oiled paper or animal skin was stretched over the open frames or a rag was stuffed into the hole. When several panes were broken around the house, one or two windows might be restored with panes taken from the bottom frame of another less useful window and then the glassless frame would simply be filled in with sod. Butcher's pictures show many sod houses that had entire windows or doors filled in with sod blocks.

Where it could be afforded, mosquito netting or wire screening was tacked over the bottom frame of a window so that it could be opened without issuing an invitation to insects, mice, and snakes.

Illustration 35

The A. L. Burger house at Gennett showed many interesting features: light sod roof, double window, horizontally pivoted window (at left), a sod fence, a willow-pole trellis, and a double-plank ridge beam. (Photographed in 1886. Nebraska State Historical Society)

Illustration 36

The Frank Owens house northwest of Callaway, Nebraska, on Spring Creek, used a half-frame window in the small addition on the gable end of the dwelling. The window is slightly ajar, showing how such windows swiveled around a horizontal pivot. (Photographed in 1892. Nebraska State Historical Society)

Illustration 37

This house photographed by Butcher in 1889 in the northwestern part of Custer County, is the only one in his collection with a triple window, that is, three window frames side by side. Note also the sod chimney. (Nebraska State Historical Society)

Illustration 38

A double-hung window was turned on its side in the Alvon Daily (or Dailey) house southwest of Milburn, Nebraska. This was a common device for 'stretching' windows in low-walled houses. (Photographed in 1888 or 1889. Nebraska State Historical Society)

Illustration 39

Although the Henry Holm house had only a one-beam roof, it also had a fine, sod-covered porch. It is hard to discern in this photo, but there is a window set directly beside the door. (Photographed in 1888. Nebraska State Historical Society)

Illustration 40

The J. N. Bates L-floor soddy in northern Custer County had bevelled outside window casements to admit more light. Many sod houses had similar bevels inside. (Photographed in 1888. Nebraska State Historical Society)

Illustration 41

This is one of the largest and handsomest houses pictured in the Butcher collection. It stood on the McCaslin land near Rose Valley. Its opulence is evidenced not only by its size but also by the large window panes, the shingled roof, and the dormer windows, that carried light to the second-floor sleeping rooms. Note also the double window to the right and the boards imbedded midway up the walls, which served to strengthen and stabilize the sods. (Photographed in 1887. Nebraska State Historical Society)

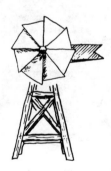

Doors:

It was less efficient to place a door in the center of the gable end of a sod house, but seventy-one of the seven hundred thirty-six sod houses pictured in the Butcher collection used this door position, seen, for example, in illustration 43. This left the door unprotected from rain and snow and cut out a supporting wall under the gable peak where weight and stress were greatest. Fifty-eight others put the door in the gable end but to one side, nearer the side wall; see, for example, illustration 53.   Three hundred eighty-nine doors were centered on the eave side of the house, and ninety-one others were to one side of the eave wall. The remainder had doors on both eave and gable ends or had them placed at variant places in the walls of L-floor or T-floor sod houses.

Eighteenth and nineteenth century frame and brick houses all over the United States often sported double front doors, that is, two front doors side by side but opening into two different rooms in the house; some sod houses reflected this same elegance. This permitted visitors to enter directly into the "good room" or parlor without going through the living rooms or kitchen.   The parlor was a sacrosanct room, always kept neat and tidy; manure-covered, muddy boots never trod on its carpet, for they had to enter by way of the other, kitchen, door. Houses that sheltered two families sometimes had two doors leading into two self-contained compartments separated by a full wall, in the style of today's duplex.

The doors themselves were made of three or four planks joined by several crossbars. Only occasionally did one see a store-bought door; only one picture in Butcher's collection shows a door with a window in it. A few doors were protected by screen doors or porches —a sod awning set on two posts.

A popular device for excluding cold drafts every time the door was

opened into the one room of a sod house was a small anteroom built around the front door. Anyone entering the house could step into the small entryway, close the outside door, and then step into the soddy itself. This was also a handy place to hang coats and canvas for beating out prairie fires. An entryway of this type can be seen in illustration 42.

At least one pioneer recalled an unusual use for the old plank door. When there were too many visitors to seat around the small kitchen table, he unhinged the front door, set it over the small table, and covered it with a tablecloth to form a banquet buffet.

Illustration 42

Although this photograph was selected particularly to illustrate the sod entry-way and plank-sheathing, it is also interesting in that it stood on the Mitchell Ranch on Clear Creek where the infamous Mitchell and Ketchum-I. P. Olive troubles took place. It is also said that this house was built across the boundary of two claims to satisfy the requirement for a "dwelling place" on both claims. (Nebraska State Historical Society)

Illustration 43

The construction of the plank door can be seen very clearly in this Butcher photograph of the W. R. Thompson L-floor house in northwest Custer County (1888). The Thompson house was one of the few to have shutters. The toy wagon was a common plaything on the plains and even in those days boys managed to break their arms. (Nebraska State Historical Society)

Ornamentation:

The sod house generally reflected the austerity of the scenery and life of the plains. The houses were severe and unadorned. Except for the natural embroidery of prairie flowers growing in the yard and on the soddy roof, there was little decoration that was not functional. Mrs. Clarence Carr recalled of her Dawson County sod house,

My mother was always throwing flower seed up on our roof; they would bloom out in damp weather.

Illustration 45

And Sarah Smith, in a letter dated May 10, 1879, asked her sister, Elmira Tibbets, who lived in Maine, to send her a packet of dandelion seeds to bring some color to her sod house in the town of Western, Nebraska. (Another letter written by Sarah Smith, contributed by Mrs. Rosalie Fuller, is reproduced on pages 131-133.)

Three photographs from the Butcher collection show small bundles of dried ears of corn—perhaps colorful Indian corn—hanging near the front door of a sod house. Corn was also dried for food, but this small quantity and the fact that it hangs near the door suggest an attempt at decoration in the same way as do the three ears of dried corn that traditionally hang on house doors in Pennsylvania and New England. An example of this decoration can be seen in illustratior. 45.

Without question the most common decorations were deer, antelope, and elk horns spiked above the door or on the ridge pole, thrown up onto the roof, or stacked in the yard. There they could be used for drying clothes, they were evidence of the hunting prowess of the man of the house, they provided a welcome change in texture, and the children liked to play with them.

[*While my father went back East to get the rest of the family*] *I was left with the Caswells. While I was staying with the Caswells I entertained myself by playing with the elk and deer horns which Mr. Caswell had gathered up here and there on the prairie. He had a pile about ten feet across and seven or eight feet high, some of the elk horns measuring as long as five feet.* (Roy Sage, Pioneer Stories)

Besides being in some ways useful, the horns were also simple decorative motifs. Eighty-three Butcher photographs show horns and antlers. For examples, see illustrations 46, 47, and 49.

Illustration 46
The ends of roof rafters can be seen about two feet below the eave edge, which suggests that the roof of this house was very thick indeed. The children's rocking horse and broken wagon were typical of pioneer playthings and like so many houses, this one too had a rack of elk horns. (Northwest Custer County. Photographed in 1890 or 1891. Nebraska State Historical Society)

Windows often sported cans of potted plants, inside and out. A handful of soddies had a trellis in front of a window—usually made of willow poles bent and tied with binder twine or wire—on which could climb an ivy or morning glory vine. One house had a horseshoe nailed over the front door. In general it must be concluded, however, that sod house life was dedicated more to survival than to aesthetics.

INTERIOR DESIGN:
Interior partitions:

Like the outside of the sod house, the inside was also a model of simplicity. Most houses had but one room; when some minimum of privacy was necessary—for a visiting teacher or preacher, for example—a canvas or muslin sheet was hung across the end of the room. Occasionally new inner sod walls were added, but these were always a source of trouble because they settled unevenly and were never completely bonded to the outer walls. It was far easier to add a new room to the old house, as at least Thirty-three per cent of the houses pictured in the Butcher collection show. Even though interior walls were thinner than outside walls—they usually were only one to one and one-half feet, that is, one brick, wide—such a wall still took up too much room in a sod house whose dimensions were only twelve by fourteen feet.

Floors:

Most soddies had a dirt floor, packed and tamped to a concrete hardness. When it got a bit dusty—during a dance, for example—the sod-house wife sprinkled the floor with a bit of water. Some housekeeping problems were unique to the sod house. Beatrice Olver of Hastings, Nebraska, tells in *Sod House Memories,* I, how her aunt had to haul water from the nearest neighbor's well — a mile away. Her only container was a two-quart jar, until somewhat later she acquired a covered coffee pot that would hold more and make the trip more worth the effort.

Sometimes sand or gravel was mixed with fine yellow clay and the floor was plastered with this, but it was not much of an improvement over the tamped earth technique, for it cracked and peeled off the floor.

The model soddy had a board floor, and some aristocratic sod-house wives could boast that they had never lived in a dirt-floor soddy. Such fortunate wives sprinkled a straw pad over the boards that were held up from the ground by two-by-four runners, then tacked down a carpet or rug to cover the rough planks. It took a while to beat the straw down to an even mat, but the result was the purest kind of pioneer luxury.

In those days we did not have any such things as rugs. We tore the old wornout clothes, dress skirts, shirts and aprons into small strips and sewed them together and wound them into a big ball. Then we would buy carpet warp of some pretty colors and have carpet woven out of the rags. It would be woven into strips one yard wide and as long as the room. These strips had to be sewed together by hand and then you had a carpet large enough to cover all the floor. Some people put straw under the carpet before it was tacked down to the floor. (Mrs. W. H. Hodge, Pioneer Stories)

Walls:

Inner surfaces were shaved smooth with a sharp spade. Because the corners were not particularly useful and because they were dirt and dust collectors, they were rounded off, leaving them easy to clean and plaster. It was customary to let the walls settle for five or six weeks (or even as long as two years) before plastering them to prevent excessive cracking and peeling. If a commercial plaster could not be afforded—and that was the usual case—fine yellow clay was mixed with water and fine sand or ashes into a thick soup and painted onto the walls.

Illustration 47

Here can be seen many common features of the Nebraska sod house — windmill, lean-to addition, transplanted saplings, elk horns, doll, and dogs — and some less common features — shingled roof, sheathed gable ends, and second-story. (E. G. Larson home, Custer County, Nebraska. Photographed in 1888. Nebraska State Historical Society)

This plaster could be whitewashed or papered with newspapers or commercial wallpapers. A very few houses had wooden wainscotting or were sheathed with "blue plaster board."*

Only the crudest sod houses had unfinished inner walls, for, without some kind of hard finish, it was simply too easy for snakes and fleas to make a home in the walls and enter the house at will. Al-

*I have been unable to determine the meaning of this term.

though there are very few interior pictures of sod houses, the frequency of plastered interior walls can be approximated by viewing the number of houses with bits of plastering showing at the outside door and window wells; see illustrations 51, 64, and 65, for example. Thirty-six per cent of the Butcher photographs show clear indications of interior plastering.

Ceiling:

Just as the walls were seldom left uncovered, the ceilings too were rarely left open to the rafters. The most common covering was a white muslin sheet tacked to the horizontal chord beams and wall plates. Of course, the muslin improved the general appearance of the house in that it concealed the rough beams, brush, logs, poles, and grass roots, but its real function was to keep sand, dirt, sticks, bugs, and snakes from dropping down necks, onto the bed, or into the soup kettle. Its light color also helped keep the inside of the house illuminated and airy. After a few months or weeks, the muslin became quite soiled (especially when spring rains dropped globs of mud onto it) and then it was taken down and laundered. It presented somewhat of a fire hazard but its advantages were worth the risk.

If muslin was not available, housewives used canvas for their ceiling; it was not as attractive, but it served the same function. H. L. Badger of Fillmore City recalled (in *Collection of Nebraska Pioneer Reminiscences*) that in his family soddy a canvas wagon cover was stretched under the roof to stop the rivulets that found a way through the sod roof.

Avalo Vannice remembered that heavy brown paper was used for the ceiling in the sod house her father built near Broken Bow, Nebraska (in *Pioneer Stories*). Of course, no ceiling could be built in the frequent soddies that had no chimney for the stove or fireplace: the smoke drifted up to the roof and found its way out a hole made near one of the gable ends or through one of the many cracks where water came in when it rained.

If there was no ceiling below the roof, planks were often laid across the horizontal chord beams or from wall plate to wall plate to form a platform where all sorts of household goods were stored. In a one-room soddy, where space was at a premium, such an attic was a very useful place.

All roofs leaked occasionally and every ceiling let through its defenses an errant bug or mouse. And, of course, smoke penetrated everything. Therefore, to provide a secure second cover for Sunday clothes and the few precious keepsakes with which the pioneers maintained a connection with the world of "civilization," many houses had a wooden (usually cedar), completely enclosed closet or wardrobe which functioned as a separate "safe" room within the soddy. It preserved for the pioneer his only luxuries and finery.

Cost:

Although it is obvious that the sod house was cheap to build, prices did vary widely according to the amount of materials purchased commercially. In terms of time, it took about a week to build a modest sod house; years, however, could go into the construction of virtual castles like the Haumont house seen in illustration 6.

Clarence Lenstrom remarks in *Pioneer Stories* that, when his father was through building his dugout near Sargent, Nebraska, he had only three cents left to his name.

In the same publication Charles Swanson tells how he handled the financing of construction of his house.

Illustration 48

This photograph shows many notable features: a pyramid roof, two bird cages hanging from the eaves, a shed-roof on an out-building, and a frame barn. (Photographed in 1890 or 1892. Nebraska State Historical Society)

Illustration 49

One of the constant hazards to the sod house was scratching cattle. On the treeless prairies, a house corner was frequently a very tempting spot to rub an itchy hide and so many barns, houses, and schools fell beneath the assault of galled cows. One way to avoid the problem was to box the house corners with planks. Note also the lean-to porch, the horns on the roof peak, and the sod-and-plank steps leading up to the door on the right. (C. N. Buck, north of Broken Bow, originally the home of U. C. Richardson. Photographed in 1886. Nebraska State Historical Society)

Illustration 50

The Newbecker house near Sargent, Nebraska, had a pole roof and a door to one side of the gable end. A cellar door can be seen clearly to the right of the picture and the girl is one of the many pioneer children to be pictured holding a favorite doll. (Photographed in 1886. Nebraska State Historical Society)

Illustration 51

The heavy round chimney on the Jacobs house northwest of Broken Bow was actually an ordinary stove pipe encased in sod and covered with clay plaster. Note the very heavy roof beams and the double window. (Photographed in 1889 or 1890. Nebraska State Historical Society)

I slept in my new house one night. Then I swung my hatchet, spade, and blanket onto my back and started south looking for a job, and landed one that afternoon with Aleck Nelson, who lived at the south side of Cummings Park. My salary was $16 a month. With the first two months' wages I paid C. K. Hall for the breaking [of the sod], and after working for two more months I sent to North Loup for some lumber for a door, door frame, window frames, two small windows, a short, wide board for a table, and a fence board for a bedstead. I intended to use plum brush for the legs and for slats to complete my bed. I bought from R. G. Carr of West Union my kitchen supplies, consisting of two tin plates, two tin cups, two knives, two forks, a coffee pot and a cast iron skillet with a lid. These he sold as bachelor supplies for $1.

Elder Oscar Babock, a Seventh-day Baptist minister of North Loup, Nebraska, gave $2.78½ as the cost of a fourteen-foot square dugout in 1872. He itemized the cost as follows:

One window (8 x 10 glass)	*$1.25*
18 feet of lumber for front door	*.54*
Latch and hanging (no lock)	*.50*
Length of pipe to go through roof	*.30*
3 lbs. of nails to make door, etc.	*.19½*
Total	*$2.78½*

(Everett Dick, Sod-House Frontier)

We built a small sod shanty, which when completed, cost one dollar and twenty-five cents. One dollar was for the window and twenty-five cents for some one-by-fours to make a frame to tack some canvas belting on for a door, using some belting for hinges. (Roy Sage, in Pioneer Stories.)

And finally, Elmer Thomas of Hastings, Nebraska, reports in the second volume of *Sod House Memories* that his father as treasurer of a school district recorded that the cost for building and equipping a thirty-two by eighteen-foot school house was precisely $31.25.

The sums seem remarkably modest to us today, but to sod-house pioneers the investment was major. When Clarence Lenstrom's father put everything down to his last three cents into that dugout, he was saying, "Here I stay."

Variant Forms:

Illustration 52
This house, owned by Z. Perry near Merna, Nebraska, is one of the few salt-box types in the Butcher collection — that is, the back wall is lower than the front and the back slope of the roof is much longer. Note also the double front door. (Photographed in 1886. Nebraska State Historical Society)

The Salt Box

Up to this point only common one-floor sod houses have been discussed, but two-story sod castles like the Haumont house, story-and-a-half Cape Cod styles, and New England salt-box styles were also built. Sod did not lend itself well to multiple-storied houses however because of its soft consistency. Most of the salt-box styles arose when a short lean-to was added to the eave side of an extant house—as can be seen by the obvious seams between the "old house" and the new addition—but it is not altogether unlikely that some were built in the salt-box style, for it is an efficient way to have second-story rooms while still presenting a low profile to prevailing winds and two floors of windows to the sun. Thirty-seven salt boxes are pictured in the Butcher collection, many of them not true salt boxes, being only one story high.

Many Nebraska sod houses had this type of profile. Since it is only one story high in front, it is not a true salt box, which is usually one and one-half stories high. This house has a barely discernable line which shows that the lean-to has been added to the back eave. The small window in the lean-to is one frame from a double frame, twelve-pane window set on its side. Many sod houses had three beams supporting the roof, like this one, for example.

The Dugout:

Illustration 53

Most sod houses were, as mentioned above, to some extent, dug-outs, but some were more obviously *dug out*. An examination of photographs 53, 54 and 55 will explain this point quite clearly; they seem to be more of a hole than a walled house. Their construction differed little from that of the sod house, except that it involved more digging than sod laying. The roofs were usually more primitive, because the house was more primitive. It was wetter inside, for it was below ground level, and water from the hill behind the house augmented the leaking roof and normal ground seepage. Many dugouts had ditches dug through the middle of the floor, out the front door and down the hill to a point where the water could freely run out, and many had ditches on the hill above them to divert the rivulets that might bring gallons of water through the back walls.

Some dugouts were mere holes dug back into a gully wall. While the sod-house dweller frequently had to worry about snakes and mice dropping from the ceiling, the dugout owner's problems came in a larger size: he had to worry about the unexpected entrance—through the ceiling—of a cow or night rider who accidentally stumbled onto his roof.

When the new sod or frame house had been completed, the old dugout became a fruit or storm cellar or an animal shelter. Few pioneers reveal in interviews or memoirs an affection for the dugout.

Illustration 54

While other sod house dwellers had to worry about mice, fleas and snakes dropping from the ceiling, the dugout builder also had to contemplate cows and night-riders straying out onto — and through — his roof, as this picture graphically shows. Watermelon was a welcome delicacy and grew well on the plains. Even a girl in her best finery could be photographed without her shoes. (Nebraska State Historical Society)

Outbuildings:

Sod was not restricted to the building of homes. Barns too were built of sod and some of them reached gigantic proportions. Sheds and barns were not usually built with the care reserved for the house, of course, and roofs were often quite crude; several Butcher photographs show barns with thatched roofs (see illustration 000, for example). Some barns were nothing more than open arbors of brush piled atop four supports and set against a hillside, much like the modern farm's loafing shed. Because of their flimsiness, barn roofs were even more susceptible to being blown off than were house roofs, and one could legitimately question whether they did indeed supply much protection for the animals when winter snows began to blow.

Pioneer Charles Letton awoke one morning to find that a blizzard had struck during the night. He managed after a struggle to push the house door open and dig up through the drift blocking the entryway to the house. Upon making his way to the animal shed, he found that it too had been drifted shut.

On crawling into this I found that during the night the snow had drifted in around the horses and cattle, which were tied to the manger. The animals had trampled it under their feet to such an extent that it had raised them so that in places their backs lifted the flimsy roof, and the wind carrying much of the covering away had filled the stable with snow until some of them were almost and others wholly buried, except where the remains of the roof protected them. (Mrs. Charles Letton in Nebraska Pioneer Reminiscences.)

One of the surprising conclusions reached in the study of the Butcher collection was the very high incidence of frame barns and outbuildings. Forty pictures clearly show frame outbuildings and since most of the pictures show a panorama of less than 180 degress of the farm, there is the distinct possibility that more than twice this number have frame buildings in addition to the sod house. In the face of this fact, a question immediately arises: if there was sufficient lumber for a barn and money enough to buy it, why was wood not purchased for the construction of a frame house? There are several answers to the question and probably all of them are to some degree correct. First, the barn was always the second building to be constructed; a man housed his family before he concerned himself with the livestock. This meant that there was likely to be more money, more available lumber, and more time for building at the later date when the barn was erected.

Illustration 55

This panorama of the Joseph Matthews homestead shows many interesting features of the pioneer farm. Near the house was a cellar dug into a hillside, a simple pole winch was used to draw water from the barrel-well, and, although the house was made of sod, the shed, cribs, fence were made of cut lumber. Costarah Matthews held her pet cat for the family portrait. Note the fine stand of corn in the background. (Photographed in 1886. Nebraska State Historical Society)

Illustration 56
The Ros Anderson farm in East Custer County (1888) offers another example of the obvious availability of wood — here used in the fences and barn — and the farmer's choice of sod for his house. One section of the pen to the far left of this picture is made of sod. (Nebraska State Historical Society)

Then the question becomes, why did they not build a frame house and use the old sod house for a barn? The most probable answer to this, and therefore to the previous question, is that the barn necessarily was bigger than the soddy. But this answer also begs the question, for the soddy could easily have been enlarged.

Two very interesting conclusions can be drawn from these facts. First, the sod house was more desirable than a frame; second, it became a tradition. The soddy's most basic and desirable advantages were not shared by frame construction: sod houses were rock solid, fire proof, naturally insulated, and impervious to the bitter prairie winds; frame houses were not. Not until resources and techniques were developed to bring the frame house to the comfort level of the sod house did people begin to build more functional frames. Even then sod was sometimes piled around the outside and lean-tos were built of sod.

I think it was a good thing people in those days had sod houses to live in; with no more fuel than they had, they would have frozen in a frame house. Those that had frame houses hauled coal from Grand Island or Kearney [to Custer County, twenty-five to one hundred miles]. (W. H. Hodge, in Pioneer Stories.)

Our dugout was so warm that during the blizzard of 1888 we sat in it and let the fire go out. (Mrs. Myrtle Chapin Herrick, in Pioneer Stories.)

The out-buildings were wood. The barn was covered with tin later on, but the cattle and all animals [had] winter coats heavy enough to take care of themselves. Some people thought the frame house was not warm enough for a family to live in. (Mr. and Mrs. Clarence Carr)

Illustration 57
Here is a fine example of the use of lumber and frame construction for out-buildings while sod was still used for the house. Butcher's label for this photograph is not clear; this may be a man named A. Bachelor or simply a man who was "a bachelor." At any rate, the photo was taken in 1889 southwest of Ansley, Nebraska. The flaws on the right are cracks in the glass photographic plate. (Nebraska State Historical Society)

In addition to efficiency was the irresistible factor of tradition. Tradition is hard to turn from its course, and there were two traditions acting on sod house construction. The standard house on the plains was the sod house. Houses were *sod* houses; the exception was the house that was not sod. Frame houses were always more desirable in the mind of the pioneer, just as glass and cedar A-frame palaces are the very essence of domestic desirability today; but few pioneers could possess frame houses as few of us can possess magnificient A-frames. To some degree, settlers built sod houses because other settlers built sod houses. And this convention continued even after it was no longer necessary to build with sod because of the total lack of any other materials.

A second impulse of tradition was an enduring European distrust of and prejudice against frame construction. Even today European visitors to America are surprised by our pre-disposition for wooden houses—and dismayed, for they quite rightly wonder at the severe fire hazard, the general looseness and frailty of wood construction and the weakness of wood itself: it rots, bends, breaks, warps, burns, swells, shrinks, and demands constant maintenance. They cannot understand why we do not take more advantage of the obvious virtues of stone and brick, for there is certainly no scarcity of these materials now. Once more we are virtual captives of our tradition.

Pioneer European immigrants may have carried with them the same prejudices and therefore used sod for their houses, reserving inferior wood frame construction for their animals.

The surprising conclusion, then, is that, contrary to what we have been taught and generally believe, it was not *only* because of the absence of wood, or the lack of choice that Nebraska pioneers built *sod* houses, but also because of the efficiency of the sod house and the momentum of tradition.

Illustration 58

This combination soddy-log house was built by Frank Cozad two miles east of New Helena, Nebraska, and was photographed by Solomon Butcher. New Helena is near the cedar canyons and so the lavish use of timber is not surprising. The front window set directly beside the front door was a common feature of the Nebraska sod house; like the double window it simplified construction and admitted more light. (Nebraska State Historcial Society)

Many unusual hybrid forms of house also appeared on the Plains. For example, even when there was enough lumber or logs to build a wood house, sod was often incorporated into the walls to keep out the wintry blasts, as Mrs. Ella Trew recalled:

We built a log house on the Loup in 1880. Then to keep it warmer, Mr. Trew piled sod up against the logs on the west and north sides to protect from the cold winds and snow, of which we had plenty . . . . . (in Pioneer Stories.)

Our Shanty had been shingled with cow-hides, thrown on the roof. During the night a cold north wind whistled through the crevices between the logs of our dwelling, which had not been chinked, and we arose, took off the roof covering and pinned the hides up against the wall to serve as siding. After this, whenever it rained, we put the hides on the roof to keep out the water and when it blew we put them on the side of the house to keep out the wind—a very simple and effective device which furnished additional proof of the truth of the old saying that "necessity is the mother of invention." (H. Lomax, in History of Custer County, Nebraska.)

Perhaps some of the most unusual descendants of the soddies are baled hay houses that were built in the sandhills area of Nebraska from 1910 to 1940. They followed the general style of the sod house, piling the bricks—in this case, hay bales—for the walls. Many hay houses are still standing and serving as homes.

*Since the Spring of 1967 I have located approximately thirty build-ings in Nebraska made of baled hay. Although this form of folk arch-itecture came much later (1920 to 1940) than the sod tradition, there appear to be many similarities between the two house types.

Other Out-buildings:

The cellar was occasionally built near or in the house itself, be-cause of the obvious convenience of this location, but more often than not it was removed ten or twenty yards from the house. The purpose of the removal was to avoid in any way weakening the foun-dation soil under the heavy sod walls and, since the cellar was used not only for storage but also as a shelter during tornadoes, to set it well beyond where collapsing walls or roof might fall on the door and trap the family. The cellar was usually dug back into a bank, in which case it had a vertical door (as in illustration 55) or dug down into the ground, in which case it had a slightly inclined horizontal door (as in illustration 50).

One of the most amusing out-buildings of sod construction to be found in the Butcher collection is the dog house seen in illustration 59.

Illustration 59

That peculiar pile of sod to the left of the Rice family soddy near Round Valley is a sod dog house, and even the family's favorite potted plant had a place in the Butcher por-trait. (Photographed in 1888. Nebraska State Historical Society)

It may be stretching the point to call windmill towers and well superstructures "out-buildings," but they were such prominent features of a farm yard, because of their soaring height and wooden construction and the fact that they were visible for miles and miles, that in pioneer Nebraska they were veritable skyscrapers.

Windmills were a later addition to the farmyard; they were evidence of money spent on drilling a well, erection of a heavy frame tower, and the purchase of expensive pumping machinery. Before the windmill, water was winched from the bottom of a well or carried over long distances to be kept in a cistern—usually a barrel sunk partially into the ground near the sod-house door. Most cistern owners hauled their water with a horse and wagon, but for some it was not so easy.

Water at first had to be carried in a two-quart jar from the well of the nearest neighbor, a mile away. Then Aunt Jennie found a covered coffee tin pot of greater and better capacity for her needs. (Beatrice Oliver, Hastings, in Sod House Memories)

In summer the water was warm—and "full of animals." In winter it was frozen solid. The coming of the windmill was indeed a major factor in bringing a comfortable life for man and animal to the American Desert.

The digging of wells was a specialized skill, restricted to very few well-paid, courageous men—courageous, because the wells had to be dug by hand and many diggers died in cave-ins and by suffocation from lethal subterranean gases. Some winch frameworks were simple to the point of being primitive (see illustration 55, for example), while others were quite fanciful (illustration 62). Cleaning a well took some ingenuity, too—

111

Any of these dug wells were subject to rodents getting into by digging under the platforms. It was necessary for the farmer or owner to be watchful. Sometimes an odd smell of the water would tell him first. I remember my father taking the mirror off the wall, and looking down the well, with the sun's reflection on it. One could usually see any mouse or squirrel floating around. If this was the case a neighbor would be called to help clean out the well. My Dad would put on rubber boots and get on a large bucket with a rope fastened to it and over blocks or pulleys this rope or tackle would be fastened to the tower of the windmill. The neighbor would handle the rope and let him down into the well. Dad would put any debris in the bucket and the neighbor would pull it up and empty it until all foreign matter was removed from the well. Then he would pull up the man in the well. After the windmill pumped for a while the water would get clear and fresh.

I remember one time in the summer during harvest time when my dad saw a mouse in the well. He wanted to remove it quickly so he asked my three little brothers if one of them would like to ride in a bucket down the well. They were all willing to go but dad chose the middle-sized because he was old enough to know what to do but still not too heavy for the bucket. We all were out to see the big event. Dad let him down, carefully tied to the bucket and rope. He was to tell when he could reach the water with a dipper and dip up the mouse. In a few seconds we waited and heard him say, "I got it" and up he came, a great hero. (Mrs. Leota Runyan, Broken Bow, Nebraska.)

Illustration 60

Many farmsteads were dominated by the massive windmills, whose blades brought up the water that enabled men to live on the Nebraska desert. It is interesting to note that while there was enough lumber available to build the huge windmill frame and a frame barn, the family continued to live in a sod house. Note the three-beam roof construction, plastered window casements, and the ubiquitous bird cage at the door. Mother would probably not be so content if she knew that the colt was about to nibble on her house plants. (Nebraska State Historical Society)

Illustration 61

The barrel sunk near the front corner of this soddy was probably the cistern in which the family stored its water supply. The water would be brought by wagon from some near-by farm that had a well or pump. The interior of this house must have been quite dark, for there is only one small window in the gable end. (Nebraska State Historical Society)

Although only ten Butcher photographs show hand pumps in the farmyard, some sod houses also had pumps inside the kitchen area, and the sod-house wife who could boast a pump in her kitchen must have felt herself a queen.

Two other sod-house farmyard features deserve mention: the bell and the firebreak. Twelve Butcher photographs show bells hanging from the ridge pole, on a pole near the door, or on the windmill tower. The bell was used to summon the men of the family from the fields for a meal or it sounded the alarm at the approach of unwelcome visitors or fire. On the open prairie the bell could be heard for many miles, and a family soon learned to recognize the ring of its own bell, if the wind happened to carry the sound of a neighbor's bell to its ears.

Illustration 62
This homestead in northern Custer County had a very handsome well frame, complete with elk horns. Note also the sapling growing to the right of the house. The accordion was one of the most popular music makers on the plains. (Photographed in 1890 or 1891. Nebraska State Historical Society.

Illustration 63

The windmill tower of many sod-house farmsteads had a bell mounted on it to signal the men to come in from the fields for a meal — or to resist some danger. (Nebraska State Historical Society)

To protect the household from grass fires, one of the most common disasters of prairie life, three or four furrows were plowed around the house ten to twenty yards apart. On a very quiet evening, when the grass was dry but not tinder dry, fires would be set between these furrows and carefully controlled by men on horseback dragging wet canvas and children wielding smaller moist cloths—often canvas pants. When the burning was completed there was a wide ring of non-flammable ground between the sod house and the prairie that would in August and September become like a powder box.

The sod house was an austere reflection of an austere life. Times were hard and we can only with difficulty imagine that sod-house life could have been at all pleasant. But just as the pioneer devised sod houses to bear the assaults of nature, he also strengthened his spirit to meet the constant assaults on his constitution and resolution.

Illustration 64

Home of Ira Foster, near Anselmo, Nebraska. (1891. Nebraska State Historical Society)

Chapter 3

Sod House Life

["The Omaha"] was the name of our boat, and she was loaded to the "gunnels," as they say, with passengers and freight. In fact, all the state rooms, berths, and cosy [sic] places were taken for the women and children and men with families, the rush to Kansas, Nebraska, and further was so enormous that spring [1857]. We young unmarried fellows had to sleep on the deck on blankets, mattresses, etc., so that I early began to know what "roughing it" meant.

We were about three weeks from St. Louis to Omaha and over a week more in getting to Decatur, our famous town site; and now we were really in Nebraska and beginning to make a state. What a queer looking place it was! A more heart-broken and dilapidated set of *tenderfeet never put hoof ashore, than we were the next day after the boat was gone and we were left fairly alone miles from nowhere and nobody "to home." Instead of four stores [as they had been told to expect] there were two log trading posts . . . and as for the fifteen houses, there wasn't such a thing as what we had been accustomed to call a house in the place.*

It was the purest democracy I ever saw; no man was above his neighbor, money made no difference for few had much, and those that had could not buy the things most valuable, viz:—help and aid physically, a good temper, the faculty of assisting to pass the time, or the ability to do something in behalf of the general welfare. It was the golden age of hospitality, for the latch string of every cabin hung outside . . . .

An old friend came from the east to see me, and when he returned, he told everybody for months, "Greatest country! Why, John took me in a buggy over a hundred miles and the wheels n e v e r struck a stone and you can plow a mile without turning a r o u n d . Think of that!"

Of no future state, just as it lies out doors, without artificial aid will it again be said, "Tickle the land with a hoe and the crop laughs to the harvest." (John A. MacMurphy, "Part of the Making of a Great State," in Number One, Volume One of the Proceedings and Collections of the Nebraska State Historical Society, July 1, 1894)

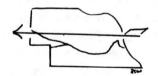

In the first place we are about as near the center of nowhere as I care to be. Imprimis, I was not cut out for a pioneer. We are fifty miles directly west from Nebraska City, which is the nearest point where one can buy a shoe-string or spool of thread. There is not enough timber to fence farms, therefore the necessity of herding stock . . . . Everybody (even, of course, I) wears a revolver or so upon his person, usually in plain sight in a belt.

The streets [of Nebraska City] are not filled with carriages and gay equipages, tho' I saw some elegant turnouts—but there are huge freight wagons on every street, at every corner; there are hundreds of oxen and mules attached to them. Often ten yoke of oxen to a wagon—six span, oftener four, of mules driven with one line. There is heard the lumbering of these "prairie schooners," the bellowing of oxen, braying of mules, cracking of the long lariats, which for me is a show of itself . . . . There is the hollowing—yelling—of teamsters, mingled with more oaths than I ever heard before in all my life together. Everybody rushing . . . . Everybody for himself . . . .

We can see a mile or more to the east from our house and two or three to the west. We often hear the trains when they are 3 or 4 miles away. The roads are very hard and there being no timber between, I suppose sounds go farther. It is curious to stand in the door early in the morning or near sunset . . . and listen to some solitary wagon that sounds as though very near, and finally be rewarded by seeing one come over the hill 3 miles away, and know that it is the one you hear. (From "Freighting in 1886, part of a letter written from the Interior of the Territory of Nebraska to the East, January 28, 1866," donated to the Nebraska State Historical Society by C. F. Bentley, Grand Island)

It was impossible for the immigrants to Nebraska to anticipate what lay before them. Not difficult, but actually impossible. In interviews, letters, diaries, official accounts, and reminiscences one encounters again and again the stunned bewilderment that overcame

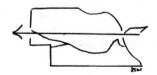

"Nebraska Gothic" — a prairie parallel for Grant Wood's famous "American Gothic." Although the potted plants and elk horns were always outside as decoration, and the canary often enjoyed the sun in the doorway, where his song still could be heard inside the house, the fancy flowered wreath and sewing machine have probably been brought out especially for this photograph — to show that civilization had indeed reached Nebraska. This is the John Curry house near West Union, Nebraska, about 1886. (Nebraska State Historical Society)

the Nebraska settler when he first saw what was to be his home. The European had of course very little preparation for the Plains; even the best informed of them simply could not adjust their thinking to accept all they had heard about the strange Nebraska desert—and this is easily understood when one notes that even today, when literacy is universal in Europe and America and Telstar joins one country to another, Americans are seldom psychologically prepared for the diminutive size of Europe, just as Europeans have virtually no concept—regardless of their education—of the vastness of this country.

The nineteenth-century Easterner, though he was familiar with American folkways, was no more prepared for the frontier of the plains. Settlers generally came from lower economic levels and so tended to have minimal educations. This of course restricted the amount of exposure they might have had to published materials, and even those who were able to read could scarcely depend on the flagrantly false reports that were being sent from the Interior: the sensationalists grossly exaggerated the hazards and poverty while the opportunists were criminal in their flattery of the wealth and opportunity to be found in Nebraska.

We, whose memories stretch back only as far as the Great Depression, are only slightly more able to grasp the pioneer's situation, for we too have been removed, like the European, from that distant land—distant for us in time however rather than space. And like the misguided Easterner of 1860 we too have been buffeted between the force that on one hand contends that Nebraska is the golden land of unexcelled beauty and scoffs at the very idea that it could have been considered a desert and on the other by those who enjoy pulling the greenhorn's leg by making things seem a good deal worse than they really are.

On arriving at Ansley I spent the night at the hotel and when I looked out the next morning I saw boxes, barrels, and anything else that was loose moving along the street. I had read about Nebraska's winds and cyclones and I felt sure that I was to be an eye witness to one during my first twenty-four hours here.

I asked [the man who ran the hotel] if the wind always blew that way. "Oh no," he said, "sometimes it blows real hard. This is just a spring zephyr." Later I asked him what was beyond those hills. "More hills" was his answer. (E. C. Spooner, in Pioneer Stories.*)*

As the hotel keeper's last answer suggests, those who weighted the scale toward the dark side were likely to be closer to the truth than those who pushed the balance toward the brighter side, for, despite all the brochures now distributed by Nebraska chambers of commerce, Nebraska *was* then a desert. Francis Parkman, who visited the central Platte Valley in 1846, was one of the most reliable chroniclers of his time; his descriptions of central Nebraska suggest the desert barrenness that later settlers encountered.

Before us and behind us, the level monotony of the plain was unbroken as far as the eye could reach. Sometimes it glared in the sun, an expanse of hot, bare sand; sometimes it was veiled by long coarse grass. Skulls and whitening bones of buffalo were scattered everywhere; the ground was tracked by myriads of them, and often covered with the circular indentations where the bulls had wallowed in the hot weather. From every gorge and ravine, opening from the hills, descended deep, well-worn paths, where the buffalo issue twice a day in regular procession to drink in the Platte. The river itself runs through the midst, a thin sheet of rapid, turbid water, half a mile wide, and scarcely two feet deep. Its low banks, for the most part without a bush or tree, are of loose sand, with which the stream is so charged that it grates on the teeth in drinking. The naked landscape is, of itself, dreary and monotonous enough; and yet the wild beasts and wild men that frequent the valley of the Platte make it a scene of interest and excitement to the traveler.

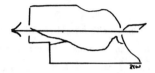

Even along the banks of the great Platte River there were only a few low bushes, an occasional tree. How far this must have seemed to be from the wooded hills of Illinois, New York, or Sweden! Yet the barrenness was only one of a catalog of new geographic characteristics to which the immigrant had to adjust.

He had little understanding of the ways of the Indians and they, despite their forbearance, had an equally difficult time translating the immigrant's culture—and, to some degree, this mutual lack of understanding exists to the present day. In general it must be said that the Indian dangers were grossly exaggerated. Although a few families died beneath the Indian knife, the Indians suffered far more atrocities and indignities from the white invaders. Indian curiosity about the ways and foods of the whites made them more of a nuisance than a danger. Those who came to understand the original inhabitants of the plains seldom suffered anything more than the loss of a thimble, hand mirror, or meal. Robert Farriter said that Custer County settlers were "more afraid of I. P. Olive and his band of cowboys than they were of the Blackfeet, who roamed the Loup Valley." For those who did fear an Indian attack however there were pioneer "burglar alarms." Mrs. George Alexander recalls in *Sod House Memories* that some pioneer Nebraskans spread newspapers on the floor in front of the door so that trespassers would rattle the paper upon entering the house and alert the household.

The distances of the prairies were staggering to the immigrant, who was accustomed to areas where every town was within sight or easy walking distance of another. Today the distances are not only shorter because more towns have been built and others have spread, but our speed also reduces to twenty minutes what would have taken a half day for the nineteenth-century pioneer. Even when he arrived at the town, which was listed as the county seat and was the largest town for fifty miles in any direction, he may have experienced some disappointment.

I shall never forget Broken Bow as we saw it on that May morning in 1883. As we came over the hill there it lay huddled below us— twelve sod houses and one frame store. To say we were all disheartened would be putting it mildly. (Mrs. Elizabeth C. Sargent, in Pioneer Stories)

Robert J. Farriter recalled that during the early years of settlement in Nebraska he lived eighty miles from the nearest doctor—a good two days' drive. He expressed the "survival of the fittest" theory in its bluntest terms: "You just had to get well or you just had to die." And he then remarked that even the dead could not rest easy, for in winter, when the neighbors could not be reached and the ground was frozen hard beneath four feet of snow, many settlers had to put any member of the family who died in a snow bank until the spring thaw.

A result of the distances was isolation. A sod-house wife might go for weeks without seeing anyone from outside her family circle. And strangers were, for obvious reasons, objects of great suspicion.

Imagine the emotions that must have coursed through the mind of the little pioneer girl who only once every month or so saw a stranger when barking dogs signaled the distant approach of Solomon Butcher's mysterious black photography wagon. Even though mother and father welcomed him and urged the children to gather around while he set up his strange equipment, many must have preferred to hide under the bed or behind the soddy curtains while Butcher took his pictures.

The barrenness of the plains and the isolation combined to induce a severe restriction of variety and quantity of supplies and equipment. The watchword was "Make do or do without," and housewives practiced the skills of salvage, improvisation, and substitution, making rugs out of the scraps of worn-out blankets and dresses, inventing ways of making "apple pie" out of soda crackers, and "stretching" coffee with parched barley or rye—sometimes with pleasing results.

The Schreyers invited us to eat and for a drink they had coffee made of rye, which they had parched in the oven and ground in a coffee mill. It was the first rye coffee I ever drank and with cream it certainly tasted good. (Albert Sprouse, in Pioneer Stories)

Settlers learned how to turn from the wealth of society to the wealth of nature. They learned how to use native prairie plants and herbs in their cooking, they learned to use rich game reserves, and, of course, they developed an architecture based on prairie sod.

Illustration 67

If you look very carefully, you can see a girl standing at the door of the soddy in this picture. Only a few visitors came across the plains and when a stranger like Butcher — with his mysterious gadgets and black wagon — came along, a bashful child might only stare from a doorway. (East Custer County. Photographed in 1888 or 1889. Nebraska State Historical Society)

Illustration 68

Here another girl — more easily seen — peeks from the soddy door. (East Custer County. Photographed in 1888. Nebraska State Historical Society)

Nature threw at the pioneer a series of natural phenomena that we have grown used to or learned to overcome. The settler however had to fight them or live with them, and if he won, he laughed at them. In the fall, grass fires swept over hundreds of miles of dry prairie grass, faster than any man and most horses could run. First—perhaps hours ahead of the fire—there was the smell of smoke, and then the distress of fleeing animals. The sky darkened with smoke and then a slim line of light appeared at the horizon. A sound like distant wind grew louder and louder. Leaving little time for back-firing or wetting down, the fire tore across the tips of the shoulder-high grass as fast as the wind could throw it ahead. As the fire swept past the sod house, the crackling and popping of the grass reached a deafening volume. Instantly the hot summer air grew searing and smoke made it impossible to breathe. Hot sparks blew everywhere; even if the fireguard kept the flames from igniting the grass around the farmstead, sparks always blew across, and frantically the family—every member—fought to save their home and their lives. Then the line of light moved away to the other horizon. The grass stalks—and the fields—lay quietly smoking. Sometimes there was the smell of burnt feathers or roasting pork. The family, choking with smoke and black with ashes, with stinging burns and reddened eyes, assessed their losses, were thankful they were alive, wondered about the fate of their neighbors down wind, and set again to work.

May 11, 74

Dear Sister, —
I have just
taken your letter from the office and
will make haste to answer it. We are all
well as yet and hope to remain so but
there has been a good deal of sickness
and quite a number of deaths here lately.
but the season is good so far Wheat is
up and looks well and Vet is ploughing
for corn and it seems as if we will have
good crops I hope so for if they happen to
fail it will put us back one year in
coming to see you anyway Vet says he
feels very anxious to come and talks a
good deal of how things will be changed
he says he could no more farm back there
now than he could fly. Andrew was in
here day before yesterday and I read your letter
to him he said it was a shame that he

had not written to you but he would do
so now. I have trided to get his wife to write
but she says she cant for she dont know what
to say I told her to do as I did say what she
thought of and let you hear from her anyway
perhaps she will write before long. I feel very
anxious to see you all and talk to you there
is a great deal I can think to say to you that
I cant write it would take to much time.
Andrew says that he thinks George would be
better off not to come for he will have to
live on his land two years before he can
own it (but if ht would come with his

family I think he would gain in the long
run there was a claim of 160 a sold in
sight of where we live for twelve
hundred dollars with no improvements
on it and they sell quite fast so you
set if he would live on his land enoguh
to hold it he would clear a good lot of
money and then could go back and live
at his ease. It has been quite a spell
since I commenced this letter and
now I will tndeavor to finish it. I told
Vet that he must write but he says I
can wrie for both of us and he will be
able to hear but I guess he will write next
time if he is well, I will send you somt
papers that are published at our county
seat and also some morning glories
I have planted the seeds you sent and
hope thty will grow all right. My baby
will be five months old next Sunday
She was born the 24 of Dec came very near
being a Christmas presant she got a
gold quarter of a dollar that night
on a tree at the school house she is
sleeping as good as can be on the bed
and Vet is marking corn ground
I wish you could just light down here
and se how much comfort we take
in our sod house for that is what we
live in and people that are worth
four and five thousand live in just such

They are very comfortable. My surname
was Thompson before I was married. You

asked if we ever heard from Louise no
we do not and should not know of
James death only we saw it in the
Muscatine Journal father takes it and
we get it from them but I must stop
and write a letter to my mothers adopted
father who lives in New Hampshire
I call him grandfather and dont remember
any other, I hope to receive an answer to

this soon and will also reply I wish I
could send you some of our nice Nebraska
scenery I think you would like it the
flowers are in bloom and the grass is
up nice and it looks beautifull but I
must stop and write more next time
Yours with Love
Sarah . Smith

Fairview Jan29th 75
Dear Sister
         I received your letter
and also your picture a long time ago
and I must ask your forgiveness for not
writing before this, but sickness of little
Sadie and then of myself, and last but
not least waiting for and opportunity to
have our pictures taken has caused my
long delay in not writing; I have asked
Vet so many times to answer your
mothers letter that he had so long ago
but he wishes me to say that if she
were here and knew now hard he had
to work she would not blame him
he has to haul wood this winter sixteen miles and that is a good days
work being a drive of thirty two miles
a day and when he gets home he is
so tired he cant write, and Sundays

he has to chop wood enough to last the
rest of the week you could harly believe
how a persons time is taken up here
if you were not present. I believe you

asked me in your letter to give you
was made and I will try to do so and
some description of how a sod house
tell you how ours is made as near as I
can, in the first place the soil is covered
in this country with a thick sod of
native grass which has to be what we
call broke, it is done with plows made
for that purpose, the sod is turned over
as if for breaking and then is cut in strips
from two to three feet long and put
on wagons and hauled where you want
the house and is laid very nearly the
same you would if they were brick only
not in mortar the wall of ours is four
feet and half thick and is thirteen
feet wide and tweny two feet
long, that is inside, the roof is made
by putting a log from one end to the

other and then laying rafters from
the log onto a plate on the sides of
the house and pinning them there
then there is a few boards nailed on
he rafters and then thin layers of sod

put on top of that and they very seldom
let the water through alhough you
migh think they would, ours has a
good fine floor in it and in the
west is one whole window and in
the sides are half windows, it is plastered
and pictures hanging on the wall in a
small quanity it would be hard to make
you believe if you did not see the outside that you were in a house made
of dirt. Vet is sitting here at the table
wih the baby on his lap and feeding
her peperment and talking to her
as if she understood every word she
heard him speak, he has a bad cold
himself, and has froze his feet this
winter and is most played out anyhow

A piece of my dress and babys dress
baby's dress is the blue. (Pin holes
sho wthat a swatch of cloth was attached
to the paper. RLW)

you will have to excuse us for not
sending you our handsome profiles in
this letter it is twenty four miles to go
where we could get them aken and
baby and I coulden go this cold weather
but we will send them before long.
I have been up to Andrews today
visiting and have had a very good time
his wife is almost sick with a headache
but it is nothing serious, she spoke of
not having written to your father since
she received his letter but said she
would write soon. And now as it is
getting late I must bring my
scribbling to an end and hope you
will deem it worthy of an answer as
soon as convenient please direct to
Fairview Saline Co. our other office is
gone out. please excuse all mistakes
in haste..
Yours truly
Sarah T. Smith

Illustration 69

The Plains behind the house were barren and vast but the house itself was rich and handsome — despite the fact that it was made of sod. The boxed corners, shingled roof, and
newly plastered or whitewashed window and door casements gave it a sharp, distinct profile, and the housewife's broom and her determined eye indicate that the inside of the
house was probably just as clean and sharp. The girl was dressed for school and carrying
her lunch pail. (Northeast Custer County. Photographed in 1887. Nebraska State Historical
Society)

The normal prairie winds were enough to tear roofs from sod houses and drive dust and snow through every crack (early settlers liked to tell about the winter winds that blew so hard that it took four men to hold a blanket over the soddy keyhole!), but even so they could not compete with the dreaded and deadly tornado. Actually, the pioneers were better prepared for tornados than we are, for the stout sod walls provided good protection and most farms had a cellar that was even safer.

No eastern or continental hailstorm could approach the ferocity of those on the plains. Men and animals died from the hammerblows of a Nebraska hailstorm.

One evening when my oldest brother was old enough to go after cows, a cloud came up quickly. Mother, who was worried about my oldest brother, watched it anxiously. Soon he came over the hill in sight. Big drops of rain started to fall; then an occasional large hailstone fell. My brother began to pick up the hailstones, not thinking of what was behind him. When the hail became very thick and large, mother saw my brother fall. She quickly grabbed the fuel basket, dumped the contents on the floor and dashed out of the door with the basket over her head. She got to my brother and the two got under the basket for protection.

My father was in the field with four horses hitched to a disc. He unhitched the horses and raced toward the barn. He reached the granary first and stopped in its shelter. One horse was close enough to the granary to be partially protected. That helped him hold on to the others while they reared against the pounding hail, but Dad held on to the reins with one hand out in the storm through it all.

In the meantime, my little brothers and I were in the house but the windows on that side of the house crashed in and glass flew all over the house. My little brothers screamed and I ran to get pillows to hold to the window. This calmed the boys.

When the storm was over, my oldest brother came in with a bump on his head the size of a goose egg. One of my dad's hands swelled to twice its normal size and my mother had a cut on her forehead that was bleeding so badly that her face was covered with streams of blood. At the sight of this my brothers and I set up a terrible scream again.

I was always afraid of hail after that. When a cloud came up, I would always ask Mother if it was going to hail. How comforting it was, when in her judgement, she would say, "No, there is no hail in that cloud." Or sometimes she would say, "Oh, this is August. It seldom hails in August." (Mrs. Leota Runyan)

Ida Walker, the pioneer mother in this story, knew that it does hail in August in Nebraska, but how she must have prayed that she was right in assuring her children, "No, there is no hail in that cloud." The terror of seeing her boy fall beneath the ice bullets, the screaming of horses and children, the flying glass, the blood and pain were a part of the experience of many pioneer wives. Even the summer sky could bring pain and death.

This hailstorm was a general calamity. The whole country suffered and many families returned, disheartened, to friends in the East. The Baptist Church was so shattered that, for its few members, it was no easy task to repair it. But soon they put it in good condition, only to see it utterly wrecked by a small cyclone the following October. The income that year from a forty-acre cornfield was one small "nubbin" less than three inches in length. (Mrs. E. A. Russell, in Collection of Nebraska Pioneer Reminiscences)

Heat and drought joined forces against the sod-buster to reduce his crop to "one small 'nubbin' less than three inches in length." Warren Fairchild of Lincoln recalls hearing about his grandfather's visit to a drought-stricken family in their sod house. When the visitor asked if crops were as bad as they seemed, the farmer, chewing on an ear of roasted corn, replied, "For lunch we just ate four acres of corn." Everett Dick notes that "from June 19, 1859, until November, 1860, not one good rain fell and there were but two slight snows in winter [in Nebraska]."

Illustration 70

There was not much time for elegance. (Mr. and Mrs. Joe Harris, West Union, Nebraska. Photographed in 1886. Nebraska State Historical Society)

Illustration 71

Life was hard on the prairie, and a few years in a sod house made a woman old before she was forty. But the eldest daughter of the Barrett Family, photographed by Butcher near Sargent in 1886, was as beautiful as the finest Boston debutante. (Nebraska State Historical Society)

The winter snows on the Plains are legendary, and the Blizzard of '88 stands as a historical monument of Plains meteorology. But disastrous blizzards also swept the prairies in 1855, 1871, 1873, 1880, and 1885. Animals died, farms failed, and families broke up furniture to feed the fire that kept them alive.

The spring rains brought torrential downpours that turned dugouts into mud baths, that washed away tons of top soil and flooded soddies along canyon walls. Even worse than the danger was the fear generated in many European hearts by the shattering, crackling Plains lightening that makes continental thunder seem like finger-snaps.

And the summer heat that withered the crops and baked the soil worked terrific hardships on the Scandinavians, Germans, and Dutch, who came from lands where people begin to faint when the temperature soars to ninety degrees.

In 1874, 1875, 1876, 1877, and 1879, when the weather cooperated to a modest degree and a good harvest was promised, a new kind of disaster presented itself.

A nice crop of growing corn was in the roasting ears when the grasshoppers came and cleaned the entire field. Before alighting they darkened the sun so much that the chickens went to roost and everyone had to light the lamps. People thought that it was an eclipse of the sun, but soon learned differently when the grasshoppers came down. In three days all their fields were destroyed. (Bert Cozad, in Pioneer Stories)

The wallpaper was eaten off the walls, clothes were stripped from the clotheslines, turnips and onions were pursued right down into the ground, supplies were sought out and devoured in fruit cellars, hoe-handles became rough as the hoppers ate away the soft parts of the wood, and harness was severely damaged by constantly moving mandibles. A few farmers tried to kill the damnable creatures with flails and fire, but the few they destroyed made little difference; and they knew that eggs were already in the ground that next year would bring a new cloud to darken the sky and strip the land.

In the fields, and often in the very walls of the sod house, lay yet another mortal danger, the rattlesnake. The bare-foot boy on the Plains soon learned to react quickly to the sound of the warning rattle, but all too often a rattler was stepped on and he struck without warning; the bite often resulted only in severe illness, but many did die. The family dog occasionally tangled with a rattler, but, though his head swelled to twice its normal size, a good dose of milk would usually clear out the poison.

Despite the dangers and hardships, life went relentlessly on. The pioneer housewife did her best to make the soddy a home. Furniture was sparse; only a few pieces were brought along to Nebraska and these often quickly deteriorated in the moist, dark air of the dirt house. As long as there was a mortgage to pay and seed to buy, there was no money in the budget for store-bought furniture. Once more it was a case of make-do. A bedstead was made of a few sticks of wood, plum brush, and boards; it was built into the corner of the house so that two walls could substitute for three legs. A couch was made of sod and covered with cloth, so that it could scarcely be recognized for what it was. Crude chairs and tables could be fashioned from packing boxes and kegs. Whenever possible, folding furniture was used to avoid crowding the tiny house even further.

That winter twelve of us lived in the [one-room] house. We had one bed up in the room and piled it nearly to the ceiling with bedding

Illustration 72
When additions were made to a soddy they were often lean-tos added to the eave-side of the house; the shallow-pitched roofs with virtually no eaves made the task a simple one. And note that it was not only the family children who went shoeless during the warm summer months! This photograph, taken in 1887, is of the Orson Cooley family near Coolyton (sic) Post Office in the northeast part of Custer County. (Nebraska State Historical Society)

[*during the day*]. *At night we made beds all over the floor. (Eva Amos, in* Pioneer Stories)

One standard item of furniture was the stove, for it was not only the center for food preparation but also the source of heat. A very few iron stoves were used; most houses were heated by a small pot-belly stove. A few unusual devices were invented to circumvent the fuel shortage—for example, the hay burner that first packed hay, weeds, and cornstalks into tight bundles and then burned the packages. Many sod-busters built fireplaces of sod, plastering the insides with the ubiquitous yellow clay-and-ashes mortar.

Beds were usually set into the corners of sod houses so that the two walls could support two sides of the bed; this system conserved both materials and labor. Over the board or pole frame was laid cross-rows of willow wands and on these was laid a mattress stuffed with prairie grass or corn husks.

My stove was of sod with iron rods across the top opening. I could bake biscuits in the skillet by placing hot ashes over the lid and keeping a slow fire underneath. I was quite comfortable with all these conveniences. (Charles Swanson, in Pioneer Stories)

The wood shortage that was so frustrating when the pioneer was trying to construct a house attained dangerous proportions in the winter when fuel was needed to sustain life. There was no wood; coal was too expensive.

141

Illustration 73
Sandhills bachelor preparing his supper. (1886. Nebraska State Historical Society)

*Fuel in early days was quite a problem. We would gather up corn-
stalks to burn and about all one person could do was keep fire. Dead
sunflowers made a good fire and burned longer than cornstalks. Cow
chips were another kind of fuel that we gathered up to burn. On
Saturday my father and we older children would take a team and
wagon and go to some neighbor's pasture. We often went to Andrew
S. Allen, Sr. He lived on a school section and had a large pasture
and kept a good many cattle, and it did not take long to pick up a
load of chips. A. H. Copsey also had quite a large pasture, which we
also visited. Father put out some willow cuttings and they soon were
large enough for fuel. (Mrs. W. H. Hodge, in* Pioneer Stories)

Illustration 74
It was more difficult for Butcher to travel in the winter, so not many of his pictures are
winter scenes. The snow on the roof of the Fellows House near Sargent demonstrates the
insulative quality of sod. Note the sled being drawn by the team of horses. (Photographed in 1886. Nebraska State Historical Society)

*. . . A standing joke in the sand hills of Nebraska ran in this wise:
A visitor asked a man how his family was. He replied that the children were all right but he hardly knew about his wife since theirs was
a passing acquaintance. They saw each other, said he, only as she
was going out with a pan of ashes and he was coming in with a bucket of cow chips, since it kept them both on the go to keep from freez-*

ing. And with all that hustle and bustle, they had no time for idle visiting. (Everett Dick in "Sunbonnet and Calico," from Kathryne Lichty's thesis, "A History of the Settlement of the Nebraska Sand Hills, Nebraska History, March, 1966)

I have also heard Everett Dick remark that many Nebraska farmers were happy to see a Texas herd bed down on their pastures, for the next morning there would be a full winter's supply of fuel steaming and drying on the prairie. He also notes that although the housewife recently arrived from the East might have only gingerly with her finger tips plucked the cow chips from the grass, in time " . . . it was only the most fastidious who bothered to wash their hands between the stoking of the cookstove and kneading of the biscuit dough!"

When cow chips ran out, hay was burned. This was prepared for the fire in one of two ways: twist it and feed it into the stove or tramp it into a hay burner. In either case the wise householder kept a pile of hay just outside the door and often, in stormy weather, the wife had to put up with a pile along the wall opposite the stove in the house. The men usually twisted the hay into "cats" as they sat about the stove in the evening, and these twists were thrown into the fire. A common type of hay burner consisted of a sheet iron vessel the shape of the old-time elliptical wash boiler. It was usually filled at the hay pile outside the door and carried inside where stove lids were removed and it was inverted over the fire box. It was the task of the woman to carry out the burner, tramp it full of hay and place it on the stove. It was one continual round of duty, and if not attended to like clockwork, the fire went out. (Everett Dick in "Sunbonnet and Calico," from an interview with Romaine Saunders, Nebraska History)

And when all else failed, when there were no cobs, hay, or sunflowers left to burn. . .

We burned corn for fuel, as coal was expensive and corn was cheap—about fifteen cents per bushel. (B. C. Jones, in Pioneer Stories)

But pioneer cooks learned to gauge the heat of burning cobs to such a fine point that they could turn out as fine an angel food cake as can be produced today.They learned to use sorghum molasses as a substitute for sugar.

Sorghum molasses was the common sweet of the settlers — so much so that the ranchers on the South Loup nicknamed them "Sorghum Lappers." (George L. Jackson, in Pioneer Stories)

And popped milo, sorghum taffy, and popcorn budding caused many plains children to think that their mother must be the best cook in the country.

POPCORN PUDDING

SOAK TWO QUARTS OF FRESHLY POPPED CORN IN THREE PINTS OF SWEET MILK OVERNIGHT. WHEN READY TO BAKE, ADD THREE WELL-BEATEN EGGS, A LITTLE SALT, AND SUGAR TO TASTE. BAKE LIKE A CUSTARD PUDDING.

I can't call up adjectives to describe the super quality of [Corn] bread when eaten with "cow butter" or ham gravy, with a glass or two of rich milk or buttermilk made in the old wooden churn. It was simply "out of this world," as the youngsters today would say. So while we did not have frosted cakes, pies with two inches of meringue, and many other musts of today, we had food which met the needs of growing, healthy bodies and we did not have to keep a bottle of vitamins from A to Z to keep us in good health.

After a night of sound sleep we would be awakened in the morning to the tune of the coffee mill grinding the coffee for breakfast, or Mother sharpening her butcher knife on the stove pipe or a stoneware crock as she prepared to slice ham, bacon, or venison for breakfast as an accompanist to hot butter-milk biscuits, potatoes, or fried mush, which made a real meal on which to start a strenuous day . . . .

There were large plum thickets and Mother would gather these plums and cook them with very little moisture, spread them on plates, etc., to dry. When dry they were leathery-like and she would roll them up, put [them] in a flour sack, and hang [them] away for winter use. (Mrs. Myrtle Oxford Hersh)

Occasionally she had to cook while one of the children held an umbrella over the food to keep mud and rain-water from dripping into the pot and there was not always enough food—or equipment—for everybody, but this hardship, like the others, was the source of some laughs too.

With company sitting about, awaiting the meal, a pioneer hostess upon one occasion was chagrined and embarrassed to find that she had so few knives. She remarked to her daughter, so that the company might hear, "My goodness Sal, where are all our knives gone to?" The daughter, failing to heed the significance of her mother's remarks, replied, "Why Ma, they're all here — Big Butch, Little Butch, Case, and Stub."

Another story I recall concerned the shortage of potatoes one year, being used as company fare only. On an occasion when Aunt Bettie Chrisman of Ansley ate dinner at our home she remarked to my father, "My laws, Genie, you all better save these potatoes for dessert." (Estelle Chrisman Laughlin, in Pioneer Stories)

Illustration 75

Edward Marsh, who owned this soddy in southwest Custer County, made certain that his wife's fancy washing machine would show in the photograph, made in 1892. This is one of the few houses that had the ridge of the addition lying crosswise to the main beam. (Nebraska State Historical Society)

Families were large and children, besides having each other to play with, were kept busy doing chores, caring for the smaller children, carrying their share of the work load. Of course, they also went to school, sometimes walking or riding many miles on horseback to get to the sod school. But there was also time for play. Butcher's photographs do not tell us much about the kinds of games they played.

Butcher's pictures do however show the kinds of toys that pioneer children played with. Of a total of seven hundred and thirty-six pictures forty-four show toy wagons—apparently the single most common toy, probably because it was a utility item, used for hauling water to the fields for the harvesters and bringing in eggs from the sod hen-house. Girls, of course, preferred dolls, and twenty of Butcher's pictures show dolls (with a total count of twenty-six dolls). Toy forms of transportation fill out to a large extent the remainder of the toy inventory; there are two each of rocking horses, tricycles, and sleds. There are also two pictures showing croquet being played, but croquet was primarily an adult entertainment. Finally, there is one toy rifle, one doll carriage, one tea set, one toy chair, and one swing— a real rarity considering the total lack of tree limbs from which to hang a swing—this one being suspended from a shed rafter. This is obviously not a comprehensive or proportionate survey, for many tin soldiers, cornstalk fiddles, and tops do not appear in the photographs because they are tucked away under the bed or are hidden in some pocket, but we can see what some of the larger toys looked like and the esteem in which they were held, in light of the fact that they were included in the family portrait.

Illustration 76

Clark Sidwell reenforced the walls of his East Rosevale dugout with buttresses of sod. With all the hardship and loneliness of the prairie frontier, little girls still managed to set an elegant table for a dolls' tea party. (Nebraska State Historical Society)

Illustration 77

H. M. Pickens' son must have had doting parents, for he had a fine wagon, a house dog (as opposed to the working farm dogs, like those seen in illustrations 78 and 85 for example), and a fancy new tricycle. (Ortello Valley. Photographed in 1889. Nebraska State Historical Society)

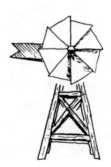

Illustration 78
This East Custer County dog-leg house had an interesting addition set into its "elbow." Two dolls can be seen in the photo and a fine sled lies on the shed roof, waiting for winter snows. (Photographed in 1889 or 1890. Nebraska State Historical Society)

Pets, like toys, often evaded Butcher's lens. Dogs had great suspicion of and little patience with the camera: sometimes the family dog is represented only by a nose sticking out of the barn door or a blur passing through the family group. Two hundred and seventy-five Butcher photographs show dogs. While only twenty-four pictures show cats, this again is not at all an exact accounting, because they were probably off chasing field mice.

Illustration 79

George Younglore's soddy, near Milburn, Nebraska, was set back into the valley wall of the Middle Loup River, clearly visible in the background. Mr. Younglore is shown holding one of his pet Maltese cats. (Photographed in 1886. Nebraska State Historical Society)

The most unexpected count in the pet category is the larger number of pet birds. Reasonably, a few pictures show dovecotes on barn or house gables, but a surprising number of houses (thirty-six) have bird cages hanging in the doorway or from the eaves, and several have two or three—for example, illustration 15. At first consideration, the thought of a canary in a sod house seems quite inappropriate, but imagine the joy that the color and sparkling song of that bird must have given the woman who spent every day in a colorless dirt house, overlooking a monotonous plain, cooking and cleaning in metronome rhythm—and taking comfort in small pleasures.

There was little family entertainment after the evening meal, which took place as the sun went down, when work was done. By the light of the stove, a candle, or a lantern the father of the family enjoyed a pipe of tobacco or read a passage from the family Bible, mother worked at her salvage sewing, began preparations for the next day's meals, or prepared the children for bed, and the children did their small chores and began to settle in for the night, because the long walk to school meant early rising.

Sometimes however there might be a game of "Old Maid" or "Animal, Vegetable, Mineral" for the children, or even something more exciting.

The young folks . . . became interested in Spiritualism. Probably the idea was encouraged by genuine lonesomeness and desire for entertainment other than their work. The spiritualism took the form of table-tipping. The table tipped out many messages. While this enthusiasm was upon them, an old man by the name of Arbuckle tramped in and stayed with them several days. . . . The table-tipping was continued while the old man was with them. A message came to them which none of them could read. The old man declared the message was in Greek, but he could interpret it just the same. The let-

ters made out the sentence, "Go to Hell." "No," said Mr. Arbuckle, "More correctly it reads, 'Go straight to Hell.' " (E. Mae Lowry, in Pioneer Stories)

One form of recreation surpassed all the others in popularity —the square dance. On a Saturday, families travelled many miles to get to a dance.

If possible these country dances were held in a cabin with a board floor, but if that was not available, the hoedown proceeded just the same on a dirt floor. The music had to be stopped occasionally, however, to sprinkle the dirt to keep down the dust. One pioneer recollected seeing a man and his wife dancing barefoot on a dirt floor with the dust flying high. Usually the unshod dancers tried to borrow a pair of boots for the special social function, however. There was little regard for time or tune as an unpolished swain grabbed the delicate woman and rushed her over the floor with the tenderness of an animal of the wilds. The dance was announced a week or more ahead of the event and people went forty miles on horseback or in big wagons and stayed until broad daylight the next morning. (Everett Dick, "Sunbonnet and Calico," Nebraska History.)

In some cases little regard was paid to the tune by the dancers simply because there was none. Most dances were to the sound of a fiddle or accordian, but if a musician—and the term was used very loosely—could not be found, a dance could be held to the music of an orchestra consisting of one man whistling and another clapping, and later in the evening a comb-and-paper virtuoso might add his talents or an aspiring musician might try his hand at the spoons.

Although there was usually only space enough to accommodate one set [eight dancers] at a time, it would be danced with gusto while the caller officiated with zest and enthusiasm. As for music,

Illustration 80
The Harvey G. Shannon house near Woods Park, Nebraska, was beginning to sag a bit when Butcher photographed it in 1887, but the fine melons on the table and the trees growing around the house suggest that there had been some success, and the fiddle held by the boy on the right shows that the successes were celebrated in style. (Nebraska State Historical Society)

there was usually some fiddler among the settlers. If he failed to arrive they danced to the music of an accordian, French harp or Jew's harp. (George Jackson, in Pioneer Stories)

The lack of space and the limited dance band apparently did not dull the enthusiasm of the dancers one bit. The dance"Ladies Bow and Gents Bow Under" was outlawed in some dance halls because of the violence it wreaked: In Eagle, a lady suffered a broken leg during this call. And "Swing 'Em by the Heels" was outlawed in the entire state, or at least this was the belief of the callers and dancers.

."After we built on the addition to our house, I sometimes gave a fiddler by the name of Gardner a dollar to come and play for a party for us to dance," said Grandpa. "We had lots of fun at our parties then just like you do now." (Mrs. R. V. Hays, in Pioneer Stories)

The dances were great places for practical jokers to practice their art, too. The wagons left in the yard were easy prey: often wheels were changed so that the two big back wheels were put on the front axle while the two smaller front wheels wound up on the back, or one of the back wheels was put on the front wheel opposite the other large back wheel and the small front wheel on the back, so that the moving wagon heaved uneasily along the rough dirt roads. Or some smart-aleck would put a piece of roofing sod over the chimney, if the fire was going, and soon the dancers would come pouring out the door, coughing, sputtering, and threatening to lynch the culprit.

At the neighborhood dances everyone in the family could be found, from the grandfather to the baby. When the younger children got sleepy they were placed in a row on the bed, where they slept soundly through all the noise of the fiddler, caller, and dancers. I have heard some old timers tell how a practical joker mixed the babies all up one night by changing some of their clothing and how it took all the next day to get them straightened out again. (Gerna Hunter Chrisman, in Pioneer Stories)

BALANCE TO YOUR PLACES AND ALL SWING —
ALL THE MEN LEFT AND PROMENADE.
JOIN YOUR HANDS AND CIRCLE TO THE LEFT.
FIRST COUPLE BREAK WITH THE GRAPEVINE TWIST —

Most of the songs sung by the pioneers—like those in the following chapter—were sung without instrumental accompaniment Instruments were rare—only ten of Butcher's pictures show musical instruments. There was little time for developing musical technique. As people sang, they worked—mending harness, mixing bread dough, twisting hay "cats" for the stove. But when an instrument was played, when music was needed for the dance, the fiddle was the instrument of the frontier. It was easily carried from one place to another, and its hard case protected it from damage. It was relatively easy to find fiddle players, which meant that tunes could be exchanged and strings could be borrowed. The broad range of textures possible on the fiddle meant that it could serve as a wild hoedown music-maker on a Saturday night and the next morning play "Beulah Land" for the church service.

Accordians and concertinas were often preferred for the same reasons; their compactness and resonant voice were very popular— a popularity witnessed by the fact that this type of instrument appears in four of Butcher's photographs.

Illustration 81

The most common way of enlarging a house was to extend its gable end, the most common form of defense was the family shotgun, and the most common music-maker was the fiddle. (Nebraska State Historical Society)

Other of his pictures show one trumpet, one baritone horn and one drum.

Several early settlers mention too that sod homes had pump organs and a good supply of sheet music, which suggests that this instrument was reserved for the sophisticated musician and art music rather than for the self-taught musician with his traditional tunes. Early in the twentieth centry traveling salesman saturated the homestead area with unusual—and generally unplayable—instruments like the ukelin, marxophone, and guitar zither; of this lot, only the autoharp gained any popularity and it is still sold and played today. (Note that the autoharp is mentioned as a pioneer music maker in the headnote to "Bugs and Fleas," page 000.)

Song played a prominent part in pioneer life, for, like the sound of the canary, a gay song was a cheap and ever-present way to bring good spirits into the sod house. Although it is difficult for us to imagine what, in the face of hardships and austerity, could have induced the sod buster to sing, his songs sometimes give us a clue.

. . . I wouldn't give the freedom that I have out in the West
For the table of the eastern man's old home.

Illustration 82
Butcher photographed the Frank Moore sod house near Sargent, Nebraska, in 1887. The house had a very heavy roof, with perhaps two layers of sod; a post was set at the gable end of the house to help support the ridge beam. The two front windows are the half-frame six-pane variety and the supporting beams above the window frames can be clearly seen in this picture. The well is a common and simple winch type. (Nebraska State Historical Society)

Illustration 83

Although it is an obvious fact, we often forget that pioneer businesses were also housed in sod buildings. The above blacksmith shop was the first in West Union, Nebraska, and was photographed by Butcher about 1886. Its roof is in part lapped-sod construction and the thickness of the walls can be seen inside the front door. (Nebraska State Historical Society)

Illustration 84

This printing office, with its well kept hipped roof and double windows directly beside the front door, issued the first newspaper in Broken Bow, Nebraska, in 1882. It was eventually absorbed by the **Custer County Chief** — the publisher of this book. Note the bits of plaster showing at the window casements. (Nebraska State Historical Society)

Illustration 85

Nor were all soddy dwellers farmers. The skins hanging on the walls, the coyote-like dogs, and the long rifles identify this as a family of trappers and hunters. The plastered window casements helped light the inside of the soddy and are evidence that the inside walls were probably also plastered. The photographer's shadow can be seen in the foreground. This soddy stood at Goose Creek in Cherry County. (Nebraska State Historical Society)

Illustration 86

Not only were houses and businesses built of sod, but churches and schools too. Like everything else in plains life, the educational system was make-shift and primitive.

December first saw the new sod schoolhouse ready for its fifteen-year-old teacher in short skirts and long braids. The little unpainted, rickety table and equally feeble chair had been salvaged from the unoccupied sod cabin of my grandmother, Mrs. Martha Mapes; the square, wood-burning stove had been lent by Reverend William Elliot, father of W. C. Elliot of Mason City; six wooden benches had been made to accommodate not only the six pupils but the people who would come there to attend church services or community affairs. At the training school we had been taught how to make a crude blackboard by applying a compound—chiefly of soot or lamp-black—to a kind of building paper. When six feet of this had been put in place and a box of chalk purchased, the equipment was complete.

The home-made benches varied, as three had backs while three had none and the only boy, Ed Cooper, contended that he should occupy one of the most comfortable ones, so a compromise was necessary. As there were no desks, the writing lesson was a protracted one, each child in turn sitting on the teacher's chair at her table to laboriously write in his copybook.

The floor was of dirt and during the cold winter of 1884 the teacher's feet were frosted. Later a quantity of straw was put on the floor which made it warmer but proved to be a breeding place for fleas. This was not conducive to quiet study but did afford the children some bodily activity.

The privations of early pioneer life were fully shared by these early teachers. One young woman, reared in a New York home with its privacy and comfort, went to board in a home where she knew she must occupy a bed with one of the children. This was bad enough, but imagine her dismay when the first night came and she learned that only a curtain separated their side of the room from that where the hired man slept. (Isabel Fodge Cornish, in Pioneer Stories)

Chapter 4

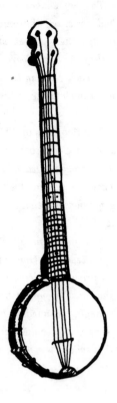

Sod House Songs

Please don't get the impression that life was just a drab existence. There was much that was interesting and beautiful. There was always the family and the great out-doors, birds, bird-nests, flowers, our nice creek where I used to play by the hour wading and trying to catch minnows and tadpoles. Often when the sun was just rising I would see mysteries in the eastern sky, which were, as I learned when I grew older, mirages.

How much I loved the evenings when father and mother would sit by our little pine kitchen table and sing from a little hymn book, the only light a little tin lamp. "Oh, that Home of the Soul," "Shall we gather at the River," "In the Sweet Bye and Bye," "Between that Fair City and Me," were fixed in my mind at that time. I recall once asking mother what a city was; she told me, and I went out in the yard and looked to the east, and pictured tall, white shiny buildings.

Father had a good tenor voice; he used to sing "Tenting Tonight on the Old Camp Ground." Years later when I sang it to him, he wiped the tears from his eyes and said, "They are all gone, but I'll never forget them." He also often sang "Down in the Cornfield," which I can almost hear as I often listen to the sound of a voice that is still. (Mrs. Myrtle Oxford Hersh)

LITTLE OLD SOD SHANTY

This song, better than any other, expresses the problems, good humor, loneliness, and faith of the sod-house settler. The last three verses, collected by L. C. Wimberely from Kate Deems of Keith County, Nebraska, in 1903, are the most eloquent of the lot, especially the last, which ends the spirited, sardonic song on a note of sincere love and hope. The tune and pattern of the chorus are based on W. S. Hays' "Little Old Log Cabin in the Lane," written in 1871. As is the case with many folksongs, this one has hundreds of claimants for its authorship—and to some degree all of these would-be authors are justified in their claim, for they are a part of the folk process which has fashioned and refashioned this song, passing it along through time from singer to singer.

This arrangement is from *A Treasury of Nebraska Pioneer Folklore* by Roger L. Welsch and is used with the permission of the publisher, The University of Nebraska Press.

I am looking rather seedy now while holding down my claim,
And my victuals are not always of the best;
And the mice play shyly round me as I nestle down to rest
In my little old sod shanty on my claim.

Chorus: The hinges are of leather and the windows have no glass,
    While the board roof lets the howling blizzards in,
    And I hear the hungry coyote as he slinks up through the
      grass
    Round that little old sod shanty on my claim.

Yet I rather like the novelty of living in this way,
Though my bill of fare is always rather tame,
But I'm happy as a clam on the land of Uncle Sam,
In the little old sod shanty on my claim.

But when I left my Eastern home, a bachelor so gay,
To try and win my way to wealth and fame;
I little thought I'd come down to burning twisted hay
In the little old sod shanty on my claim.

My clothes are plastered o'er with dough, I'm looking like a fright,
And everything is scattered round the room,
But I wouldn't give the freedom that I have out in the West
For the table of the Eastern man's old home.

Still, I wish that some kind-hearted girl would pity on me take,
And relieve me from the mess that I am in;
The angel, how I'd bless her, if this her home she'd make
In the little old sod shanty on my claim.

And if fate should bless us with now and then an heir
To cheer our hearts with honest pride of fame,
Oh, then we'd be contented for the toil that we had spent
In that little old sod shanty on our claim.

When time enough had lapsed and all those little brats
To noble man- and womanhood had grown,
It wouldn't seem half so lonely as round us we should look
And we'd see the old sod shanty on our claim.

Variant verses to LITTLE OLD SOD SHANTY:

A bumper crop of corn we raised in eighteen ninety-two;
To dress our wife in silk we thought was plain;
But we sold our corn for thirteen cents, three cents beside a share,
So the wife stayed in the shanty on the claim.

Our hogs they died of cholera, our chickens had the pip;
The baby swallowed buttons like a chain;
Our wife was married thirteen years before she saw a dime
When we lived in that sod shanty on the claim.

Yet for all the hardships we went through, we never gave up hope,
But plugged the harder till we made it gain.
For love was close beside us in all our ups and downs
In that little old sod shanty on the claim.

Illustration 87

Starving to Death on a Gov't Claim

Lane County is in west-central Kansas, but this song was sung with equal gusto and conviction throughout the plains states of North and South Dakota, Nebraska, and Kansas, because it so clearly spoke for the feelings of the whole area and described so well the trials every sodbuster encountered. Although Lane County's political boundaries restrict it to a small twenty-five by thirty mile patch of Kansas prairie, it became, as a result of this song, a symbolic representative of the homesteaders from Canada to Oklahoma, from the Rockies to the Missouri.

Today, chambers of commerce and regional patriots are offended by what appears to be a crass insult in these songs to the geographic object of their affection. But they were not often sung by the people who painted "Busted. Gone back East to live with the wife's folks" on their wagons and retreated across the Missouri. Songs like "Starving to Death on a Government Claim," "Little Sod Shanty on the Claim," and "Sweet Nebraska Land" were sung by those who stayed, who learned to laugh at hardship. Just as they exaggerated the climate in their speech and tales, they also embroidered their problems in these songs, for by doing so they were saying, "No ordinary man can make it in this desert land; I'm doing fine."

The following version—there were many—was collected in Nebraska by Louise Pound and was published in *A Treasury of Nebraska Pioneer Folklore* by Roger L. Welsch; it is used here with the permission of the publisher. The tune is "The Irish Washerwoman."

170

Frank Baker's my name, and a bachelor I am.
I'm keeping old batch on an elegant plan.
You'll find me out west in the county of Lane,
A'starving to death on a government claim.

My house is constructed of natural soil,
The walls are erected according to Hoyle,
The roof has no pitch, but is level and plain,
And I never get wet—till it happens to rain.

Hurrah for Lane County, the land of the free,
The home of the grasshopper, bedbug, and flea.
I'll holler its praises and sing of its fame,
While starving to death on a government claim.

How happy I am as I crawl into bed,
The rattlesnakes rattling a tune at my head,
While the gay little centipede, so void of all fear,
Crawls over my neck, and into my ear.
And the gay little bedbug so cheerful and bright,
He keeps me a-going two-thirds of the night.

My clothes are all ragged, my language is rough,
My bread is case-hardened, both solid and tough,
The dough is scattered all over the room,
And the floor would get scared at the sight of a broom.

The dishes are scattered all over the bed,
All covered with sorghum and government bread;
Still I have a good time and I live at my ease
On common sop sorghum and bacon and cheese.

How happy I am on my government claim,

I've nothing to lose, I've nothing to gain,
I've nothing to eat and I've nothing to wear,
And nothing from nothing is honest and fair.

Oh, here I am safe, so here I will stay,
My money's all gone, and I can't get away.
There's nothing to make a man hard and profane
Like starving to death on a government claim.

Now come to Lane County, there's room for you all,
Where the wind never ceases and the rains never fall.
Come join in our chorus to sing for its fame,
You sinners that're stuck on your government claim.

Now hurrah for Lane County, where the blizzards arise,
The wind never ceases and the moon never rise,
Where the sun never sets, but it always remains
Till it burns us all out on our government claims.

Now don't get discouraged, you poor hungry men,
You're all just as free as the pig in the pen,
Just stick to your homestead and battle the fleas,
And look to your Maker to send you a breeze.

Hurrah for Lane County, the land of the West,
Where the farmers and laborers are ever at rest;
There's nothing to do but to stick and remain,
And starve like a dog on a government claim.

Now, all you poor sinners, I hope you will stay,
And chew the hard rag till you're toothless and gray,
But as for myself I'll no longer remain
To starve like a dog on a government claim.

Farewell to Lane County, farewell to the West,
I'll travel back East to the girl I love best;
I'll stop at Missouri and get me a wife,
Then live on corn dodgers the rest of my life.

This song was found by Raymond Benjamin among the effects of his grandmother, Maybelle Clair Benjamin, when he was a student at Nebraska Wesleyan University. Mrs. Benjamin was a pioneer in the area of McCook, Nebraska. Relatives recall that the song was sung to the tune of "The Yellow Rose of Texas." I especially thank Mr. Benjamin for permission to use the song in this collection.

We call ourselves the Soddies,
We have kinship with the sod;
We're pioneers of the U.S.A.
Best Country under God.
The land it was our heritage,
We tilled it faithfully,
And trusted God to give us
Strength and ingenuity.

Chorus:
We are Soddies from the prairies,
The mountains and the plains,
Where e'er the land was Uncle Sam's
We planted there our claims.
But where once stood the old sod house,
There thrives a fertile field,
And we are here to tell the world
What made those prairies yield.

We Soddies well remember when
No fuel could be found.
Those cows they must have wondered
Why we followed them around!
No papers had we—such, the odds
For these were luxuries.
We shelled the corn and saved the cobs,
No laughing if you please.
Chorus:

We are Jayhawkers from Kansas,
We are Gems from Idaho.
Cornhuskers from Nebraska State,
Show-Me's from old Mo.

We are Wolverines from Michigan,
Gophers from Minnesoty,
We are Hoosiers from old Indianne,
Coyotes from South Dakoty.
Chorus:

You mockers from the Lone Star State,
Redbirds from little Rhody,
Roadrunners from New Mexico,
Flickers from North Dakoty,
You Meadowlarks from Oregon,
Bluehens from Delaware,
We'll all join in and here and now,
This Rally Song we'll share.
Chorus:

Illustration 88

Although the Abraham Hyatt home on Elk or Cat Creek was already beginning to show
wear at the base and needed a support on one eave end when this photo was taken in
1886, the wealth of the family can be seen in the large herd in the background, the two
brick chimneys, and the sheathed gables. The windows in the gables probably opened
into the low sleeping rooms, usually used by the family children. (Nebraska State Historical Society)

bugs and fleas

Mrs. William Lenneman of Orleans, Nebraska, contributed "Bugs and Fleas" to the Newsletter of the Nebraska Folklore Society, Volume II, number 3, Spring, 1964.

My grandfather, Solomon W. Stilgebauer, brought his family to Danbury, Nebraska, in 1875. On Sunday afternoons, or when there were guests, my grandfather would take his accordian or his autoharp and accompany his four sons, who would sing the songs of the pioneers. Just for fun the sons composed "Bugs and Fleas." One Sunday afternoon they sang it—a complete surprise to my grandfather. My father tells that my grandfather laughed so heartily that he had to quit playing the accordian. As a child I recall hearing my father sing this song many times.

The tune is that of "Little Brown Jug."

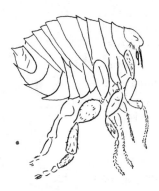

We're in the land of bugs and fleas
And golly, don't they go for me.
They bite my back and bite my breast,
They won't give me a minute's rest.

Chorus:
    Ha ha ha, don't you know,
    I am telling what is so.
    Ha ha ha, don't you know,
    I am telling what is so.

When emigration first comes in
They think this country's settled thi
But when the fleas around them stic
They begin to think it's settled thick.
Chorus:

'Twas just the other day I found
A great big flea that weighed five pound.
The top side of him it was black.
Put him 'tween my thumbs and he did crack.
Chorus:

Oh buggy land, sweet buggy land,
Whether I lie or whether I stand,
They look around and me they see,
And then they make a jump for me.
They climb my frame from off the floor
And then they bite for evermore.
Chorus:

I've scratched myself till I am sore

And still I scratch the more and more
And now my song is almost sung
For a great big flea his work's begun.

Chorus:
  Ha ha ha, don't you know,
  I am telling what is so.
  Ha ha ha, don't you know,
  I am telling what is so.

Sweet Kansas/Nebraska Land

Anyone who sings this song should be prepared for a flurry of comments, all along the general design of "you left out two verses" or "that isn't the way it goes" or "what about that part that goes

> 'The farmer goes into his corn,
> And there he stands with look forlorn,
> And to himself begins to talk,
> And sees the shoots have missed the stalk.' "

This song has developed more twists and turns than the travelling-salesman joke. It is sung not only as "Sweet Nebraska Land" and "Sweet Kansas Land," but also "Sweet Dakota Land," "Sweet Saskatchewan," and "Sweet Idaho." Originally it was based, of course, on the hymn "Beulah Land" and many versions are still sung to that tune.

The following version of "Kansas Land" is from Koch and Sackett's *Kansas Folklore* and is used with permission of the University of Nebraska Press. Although its headnotes state that it is to be sung to the tune of "Maryland, My Maryland," this version is probably to be sung to the tune of "Beulah Land," for whenever the former tune was used for variants of this song, the last two lines of the chorus were omitted.

I've reached the land of corn and beans
At first the crop looked fine and green,
But the grasshoppers and the drouth—
We'd better pull up and go south.

Chorus:

O Kansas sun, hot Kansas sun,
As to the highest knoll I run,
I look away across the plains,
And wonder why it never rains.
And as I look upon my corn,
I think but little of my farm.

If we are poor, we're not to blame.
We'll go back East and sell the claim,
And if we succeed in getting tin,*
We'll drive a herd of cattle in.
Chorus:

My hoss is poor; I cannot plow,
But I can trade it for a cow.
My wheat is thin, but let it pass,
The cow can feed on buffalo grass.

Chorus for last verse:

O Kansas girls, sweet Kansas girls,
With sky-blue eyes and flaxen curls—
They sing and dance and flirt and play
And when a boy friend comes that way
They meet him at the sod house door,
Then be with him forever more.

This first version of "Sweet Nebraska Land" is from *A Treasury of Nebraska Pioneer Folklore* and is also used with the permission of the University of Nebraska Press. It was sung to the tune of "Maryland, My Maryland," and whenever the "Beulah Land" tune was used, the first line of the chorus was changed to "Nebraska land, sweet Nebraska land . . . " and two lines were added,

> "Till Gabrie blows his trumpet sound
> To say the rain is going 'round."

We've reached the land of desert sweet
Where nothing grows for man to eat.
The wind does blow with blist'ring heat
O'er the plains so hard to beat.

Chorus:

> Nebraska land, Nebraska land
> As on thy desert soil I stand
> And look away across the plains,
> I wonder why it never rains.

There is no wheat, there is no oats,
Not even corn to feed our shoats.
Our chickens are so thin and poor,
They come and peck crumbs off the floor.

Chorus:

Our horses are of bronco breed;
They nothing have on which to feed.
We do not live, we only stay;
We're all too poor to get away.

Chorus:

The final version of "Sweet Nebraska Land" is one for the good years.   The happy verses were reputedly written by Frank Price in Atkinson, Nebraska, to celebrate the fine crops of 1895.

I've reached the land of sun and rain
Out on Nebraska's verdant plain,
Where everything grows so fast
It takes your breath as you go past.

Chorus:

Oh! Nebraska land, sweet Nebraska land,
As on the growing soil I stand,
I look away across the plain
To see the acres filled with grain,
And feel like shouting out to all,
What a hell of a crop we'll have this fall.

The wheat and oats are ten feet high,
The sunflowers reach up to the sky,
And everything has grown so fine,
It has knocked the kickers out of time.

Chorus:

Our pumpkins they are large and round,
Our sugar beets weigh twenty pound.
Our corn it is so very big,
One ear will fatten a berkshire pig.

Chorus:

Our chicken crow both night and day,
Our pigs are fat as Ed O'Shea,
The cows they give the richest milk,
And everything is fine as silk.

Chorus:

Nebraska she is now all right;
She is going to be clear out of sight.
No matter where you choose to roam,
Don't leave Nebraska for a home.

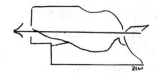

KINKAIDER SONG

The "Kinkaider Song" was a great favorite at sandhills picnics and outings. And it was with good reason that the homesteaders sang the praises of Moses P. Kinkaid, for he authored the bill that in 1904 made vast new lands in the Nebraska sandhills open for homesteading.

The tune is "Maryland, My Maryland," and this version is taken from Louise Pound's syllabus, *Folk-Song of Nebraska and the Central West*.

You ask what place I like the best,
The sandhills, oh, the sandhills;
The place Kinkaiders make their home
And prairie chickens freely roam.

Chorus:
In all Nebraska's wide domain
'Tis the place we long to see again;
The sandhills are the very best,
She is the queen of all the rest.

The corn we raise is our delight,
The melons too are out of sight,
Potatoes grown are extra fine,
And can't be beat in any clime.
Chorus:

185

The peaceful cows in pastures dream
And furnish us with golden cream,
So I shall keep my Kinkaid home
And never far away shall roam.

Chorus (for third verse):
Then let us all with hearts sincere
Thank him for what has brough us here,
And for the homestead law he made,
This noble Moses P. Kinkaid.

Illustration 89
William Pfrehm intended to make his farmstead something more than the desolate prairie all around it: note the saplings planted in the foreground. His house was well built, with framed window casements, a neatly sodded roof, and a frame addition. (Photographed in 1886. Nebraska State Historical Society)

the mortgage worked the hardest

In the late '80's and early '90's depression, graft, and government-al corruption on state and national levels, bad weather, and grass-hoppers drove the Nebraska farmer to the wall. As he had sung to express his joy, he also sang to express his anguish—and to drama-tize his protest.

No tune for the song below is indicated in the early Farmers' Al-liance publications where it first appeared and in the collections of the W.P.A. where it was collected and deposited in the late 1930's.

We worked through spring and winter,
Through summer and through fall,
But the mortgage worked the hardest—
And the steadiest of them all.
It worked on nights and Sundays;
It worked each holiday;
It settled down among us—
And never went away.

Whatever we kept from it
Seemed almost as a theft.
It watched us every minute;
It ruled us right and left.
The rust and blight were with us—
Sometimes and sometimes not.
But the dark-browed, scowling mortgage

Was forever on the spot.

The weevil and cut worm,
They went as well as came;
The mortgage stayed forever,
Eating hearty all the same.
It nailed up every window,
Stood guard at every door,
And happiness and sunshine
Made their home with us no more.

Till with failing crops and sickness,
We got stalled upon the grade,
And there came a dark day on us,
When the interest wasn't paid;
And there came a sharp foreclosure,
And I kinda lost my hold,
And grew weary and discouraged,
And the farm was cheaply sold.

The children left and scattered,
When they hardly yet were grown;
My wife, she pined and perished,
And I found myself alone.
What she died of was a "mystery,"
The doctors never knew,
But I knew she died of mortgage—
Just as well as I wanted to.

If to trace the hidden arrow
Was within the doctor's art,
They'd a-found a mortgage lying
On that woman's broken heart.

Worm or beetle, drouth or tempest
On a farmer's land may fall,
But for first-class ruination,
Trust a mortgage 'gainst them all.

Illustration 90

Harry Bryan's home near Ansley, Nebraska. (Photographed in 1888. Nebraska State Historical Society)

VOTE FOR ME

One of the classic tear-jerkers of the temperance movement was "Come Home, Father," the plea of a starving child trying to drag her father from a saloon to the bedside of her dying brother. But the cruel and rum-soaked father does not heed her plea and ignores little Benny's last words, "I want to kiss Papa good night."

In the true tradition of the broadside song and the protest singer, Mrs. J. T. Kellie, the most prolific writer of the Farmers' Alliance protest movement, wrote "Vote for Me" in the style and to the tune of "Father, Dear Father, Come Home with Me Now." Her wrath is directed, with some reason, against the railroad cartel, and indirectly toward the political parties of the late nineteenth century.

The railroads, which the farmers had hoped would be a blessing, carrying their crops quickly and cheaply to the eastern markets and returning with supplies for building the land, turned out to be instead a curse. The monopolies permitted giants like Jay Gould to charge outrageous prices, until it cost a bushel of grain to ship a bushel of grain. When the farmer turned to the politicians for help, he found them with their hands and pockets stuffed with free railroad passes; they had no interest in his problems. For the farmer it appeared there was no hope—except perhaps to bring his problem to the public attention through rallies and songs.

VOTE FOR ME: Mrs. J. T. Kellie (Tune: Father Come Home)

Oh father, dear father, come vote for me now

My clothes are so worn out and old,
You said you would get me some new ones this fall;

But now wheat and corn are all sold.
The roads took the best, the banks got the rest,

And nothing is left us at all;
We thought if we worked through the heat and the cold,

We'd have lots of new things this fall.

Chorus: Be free, for me;
      Come, father, please vote for me now.
      Oh father, dear father, come vote for me now,
      Heed not what the railroad men say,
      Of course they will tell you they love you best,
      You know that was always the way;
      Yet our sod house is old and lets in the cold,
      And Ma's always patching, you see;
      The rest of the children, their shoes are so old—
      There's no one can bring cobs but me.

Oh father, dear father, come vote for me now,
   You know that I can't go to school,
For summer or winter, year round I must work,
   And when I am grown to be a fool;
Oh, what can I do when grown up like you,
   And nothing I know but to save,
Free land will be gone and naught else can I do
   But be to the rich men a slave.
Chorus:

Oh father, dear father, come vote for me now,
    Let money men threaten or pray,
They told you last summer we all worked too hard,
    This year we are lazy they say;
Dear father, that's right, oh, what a glad sight,
    That old railroad ticket thrown down,
Now Ma will be hopeful, her heart will be light,
    I'll have clothes like rich boys in town.
Chorus:

great granddad

When the pioneers of Nebraska sang the following song about the earlier pioneers of the East, they must have known that they were also singing about themselves. Our kinship with the builder of the sod house is never more apparent than it is in this song, where we see a sod-buster asking the question, "What is becoming of the younger generation?" (Collected from Nebraska singers by the author.)

Great-grandad when the land was young,
Barred the door with a wagon tongue;
Times was rough and danger mocked—
He said his prayers with his shotgun cocked.

He was a gentleman tough and grim;
Danger was duck soup to him.
He ate cornpone and bacon fat—
Great-grandson would starve on that.

Great-granddad was a busy man:
He cooked his grub in a frying pan,
He picked his teeth with a hunting knife,
And he wore the same suit all his life.

Twenty-one children came to bless
The old man's home in the wilderness.
Doubt this statement if you can,
Great-granddad was a busy man.

Twenty-one boys and how they grew,
Tall and strong on the bacon too.
Slept on the floor with the dogs and the cats,
And hunted in the woods in their coon-skin caps.

Twenty-one boys and not one bad,
They never got fresh with their old dad,
For if they had, he'd a-been right glad
To tan their hides with a hickory gad.

He raised them tough and he raised them well.
If their feet set hold on the road to Hell,
He straightened them out with an iron ramrod,
And filled them full of the fear of God.

They grew strong at heart, strong at hand,
Firm foundation of our land.
Twenty-one boys and one grandson,
Who has a terrible time with his one.

This picture is one of the later sod-house pictures in the Butcher collection; it was made in 1904. It is also one of the saddest, for it shows Eli Armstrong about to destroy an old soddy on the Reynor property near Broken Bow. (Nebraska State Historical Society)

Author's Afterword

Many sod houses still stand in Nebraska. Some are virtually in total ruin but a surprising number are still lived in—and they are as comfortable and attractive as modern development houses. But very few new ones have been built in the traditional style since World War One and, of course, every year old ones are destroyed or collapse because of the elements. Those houses that remain deserve our immediate attention.

If nothing else, the soddy can remind us of the hardships that were endured by the people who built it and lived in it. Perhaps it can remind us of our debt to those who came before us, of our heritage. This remembrance is not so much to increase our pride as our humility, for it is by no effort or talent of our own that we have become heirs of their accomplishments. We are the product of all those who came before, who lived in the soddies—even if our parents came from Germany long after the Sod-House Frontier, as Everett Dick so aptly calls it, had passed.

The sod house deserves respect. Only a few will be saved. Despite their basic sturdiness—especially those with good roofs—they are doomed. Some will simply dissolve bit by bit in the Nebraska rains. Others will be pulled down and plowed away—because they provide an all too convenient convention hall for skunks and weasels, because they are unattractive, because . . . .

In fact, it will only be by extraordinary effort that any will be saved, because it is far easier to build a new sod house than it is to save an authentic old one. But the results are also far less satisfying. A new sod house is a mere imitation, no matter how much money, care, and research is spent on the reconstruction. A builder can take two-hundred-year-old wood, use an old plane and hammer, have nails wrought in a forge, and build a table according to an eighteenth-century plan, but the result is not an antique; it is only replica. And the same is true of the reconstruction of a sod house.

An interesting development in museum science has a bearing on this problem. More and more, in addition to historical museums, which preserve the historically significant items of a culture, and art museums, which preserve artistically important materials, Europeans have been establishing folk museums, the purpose of which is to preserve average, traditional features of a village, area or country.

These folk museums are usually open-air displays, where typical houses, barns, and commercial buildings are brought to a location and are arranged in historically consistent contexts. Homes, farms, and stores are restored to a condition exactly as they might have been at one particular time in the past. Often traditional life is portrayed as it was within these buildings: costumed women cook in the kitchens, for example, and men grind grain at the water-driven mill. Some folk museums permit visitors to move about within the exhibits, to hold—and even to manipulate—the tools, to sample cakes that are hot out of the oven and made of hand-ground flour, or to sit on the furniture. Weekends are highlighted with dance and song festivals—always of traditional materials, lectures, and programs of particular interest to museum visitors, and special exhibits.

The folk museum movement has spread to a small degree to this country, and is especially evident in the East. The Farmers' Museum at Cooperstown, New York, Mystic Seaport in Massachusetts, and New Salem in Illinois are in part open-air folk museums, and there has even been some discussion of establishing such a museum in Nebraska—at Dana College in Blair, Nebraska, for example, at the Stuhr Museum in Grand Island or at the State Historical Society in Lincoln.

The problem of moving entire buildings—old buildings, especially—seems an impossible task, but techniques have been developed that make even the relocation of brick and stone buildings a manageable assignment. Sod too would provide its special problems, but it would not be impossible to transport a soddy, and later generations would assure us that the effort was well worthwhile. The cost would be little more than that of the materials and labor spent for less satisfying imitations.

Several courses of action are open to those who support the preservation of our pioneer past. 1) They might support their local, county, and state historical societies in all of their activities, for it is through these organizations that the restoration of a sod house and establishment of a folk museum is most likely to begin. 2) They could urge these societies to take an interest in traditional folk materials and initiate action toward the preservation of a local sod house. 3) They might suggest restoration of the house, but only under the guidance of a qualified, competent historian, museum curator or student of folk architecture. This caution must be stressed because of the ruinous results that are frequently brought about by the well-intentioned but misguided amateur restorer. 4) They might aid their local and state historical societies by photographing sketching, measuring, and tracing histories of sod houses and by depositing their findings in archives where they can be made available for future students of Plains life. All letters, for example, that have described for me the construction of the sod house and life in it have been deposited in the archives of the Nebraska State Historical Society. 5) Finally, any letters, photographs, or histories of sod houses may be sent to me, and I will be glad to see that they make their way to the appropriate archives.

The successful investigation of the Nebraska sod house will depend upon the efforts of all Nebraskans who are interested in our rich heritage. I therefore hope that I have presented the case of the sod house as it deserves to be presented. If there is any fault in the argument, it must be my own and not the soddy's, for its character and validity are undeniable.

Bibliography

Any book dealing with history—indeed, virtually any book—must rely heavily on the work of others who have published relevant studies. One of the purposes of documentation and bibliography is to give recognition to previous researchers; there are some scholars however whose contributions to *Sod Walls* demand more than a footnote or bibliographic entry. James Olson's *History of Nebraska* (University of Nebraska Press; Lincoln, 1955, 1966) was the standard reference for the historical data in *Sod Walls*. Everett Dick's excellent books, *The Sod-House Frontier* (D. Appleton-Century Company; New York, 1937) and *Vanguards of the Frontier* (D. Appleton-Century Company; New York, 1941), and his article "Sunbonnet and Calico, The Homesteader's Consort" *(Nebraska History, 47:1,* March, 1966, Lincoln: pp 3-13) provided reliable accounts of conditions during the homesteading of Nebraska, and I have taken advantage of Professor Dick's excellent taste in the selection of quotations from interviews, articles, and theses. Frances Alberts and the Nebraska Sod House Society deserve the thanks of all of us for their efforts to collect and publish pioneer reminiscences in *Sod House Memories,* volumes I and II (Hastings, Nebraska, 1963, 1967). Emerson R. Purcell's impressive collection of Custer County tales, *Pioneer Stories of Custer County, Nebraska* (referred in the text of *Sod Walls* as *Pioneer Stories)* told in the words of the pioneers themselves, yielded the bulk of previously published accounts used here; it must also be noted that Emerson Purcell's son, Harry Purcell, is continuing his father's efforts to record the struggle of the Nebraska pioneer by publishing *Sod Walls,* re-issuing *Pioneer Stories of Custer County, Nebraska,* and frequently printing pioneer accounts in the *Custer County Chief* of Broken Bow, Nebraska.

Also used were the following:

Bang, Roy T. *Heroes without Medals* (Warp Publishing Company; Minden, Nebraska, 1952.)

Barns, Cass G. *The Sod House* (Madison, Nebraska, 1930).

Cox, W. W. "Reminiscences of Early Days in Nebraska," a paper read before the Nebraska State Historical Society, January 11, 1893, in *Transactions and Reports of the Nebraska Historical Society*, Volume V (Lincoln, 1893).

Daughters of the American Revolution. *Collection of Nebraska Pioneer Reminiscences* (Cedar Rapids, Iowa, 1916).

"Freighting in 1866, Part of a Letter Written from the Interior to the East, January 28, 1866," donated to the Nebraska State Historical Society by C. F. Bentley, Grand Island, Nebraska.

Gaston, W. L., and A. R. Humphrey, *History of Custer County, Nebraska* (Western Publishing and Engraving Company; Lincoln, 1919).

La Flesche, Francis, and Alice C. Fletcher, *The Omaha Tribe*, extract from the twenty-seventh annual report of the Bureau of American Ethnology (Government Printing Office; Washington, D.C., 1911).

MacMurphy, John A., "Part of the Making of a Great State," in *Proceedings and Collections of the Nebraska State Historical Society*, Volume I, Number I, second series (Lincoln, 1894).

Morton, J. Sterling, *Illustrated History of Nebraska* (Jacob North and Company, Lincoln, 1906).

Appendix

I am indebted to the following people for the help, information, photographs, and precious memories of sod houses and sod-house life.

Abbot, Earnest
Almeria, Nebraska

Anderson, Ralph
Cozad, Nebraska

Armstrong, Darrel and Darlene
Big Springs, Nebraska

Aydelotte, Margaret
Arnold, Nebraska

Baird, William

Ball, Mrs. Henry
North Platte, Nebraska

Benjamin, Ray

Callur, J. N.
North Platte, Nebraska

Capek, Dave
Milligen, Nebraska

Carr, Clarence
Kearney, Nebraska

Cooksley, George
Berwyn, Nebraska

Cox, R. K.
Purdum, Nebraska

Cummins, Nancy
Falls City, Nebraska

Dady, Mrs. Hazel
Ansley, Nebraska

Davis, Horace
Lincoln, Nebraska

Dewey, Rosa
Ansley, Nebraska

Drake, Girtie Hoshaw
Twin Falls, Idaho

Eacker, Mrs. Gilbert
Broken Bow, Nebraska

Ellis, O. C.
Omaha, Nebraska

Farritor,
    Mr. and Mrs. Morris
Broken Bow, Nebraska

Fochtman, W. J.
Callaway, Nebraska

Fuller, Rosalie
Lincoln, Nebraska

Hansen, Rueben
Minden, Nebraska

Hatting, John
Lexington, Nebraska

Haumont, Jules
Round Valley, Nebraska

Haumont, Steve
Broken Bow, Nebraska

Hemmingsen, Sharon
Auburn, Nebraska

Henderson, Maude
Whitman, Nebraska

Hersh, J. Dean
Dunning, Nebraska

Holmes, B. V.
Broken Bow, Nebraska

Huhman, Mrs. Bud
Broken Bow, Nebraska

Hurn, Opal
Broken Bow, Nebraska

Jones, Lawrence L.
Seneca, Nebraska

Kennelbarger, Mildred

Kiker, Mrs. J. C.
Yuma, Arizona

Koch, Ethel F.

Kruser, George
Arnold, Nebraska

Lawlis, Mrs. Albert
Broken Bow, Nebraska

Lynch, Willard
Thedford, Nebraska

Mason, Mildred
Loveland, Colorado

McCaslin, D. H.
Broken Bow, Nebraska

McGaughey, G. W.
Montrose, Colorado

Miller, Niels
Herman, Nebraska

Murphy, Mrs. Gene
Agate, Nebraska

Myers, Jim
Broken Bow, Nebraska

Myers, Mrs. Mabel M.
Eddyville, Nebraska

Norland, Orville A.
Broken Bow, Nebraska

O'Mara, Earl
Eddyville, Nebraska

Owen, William H.
North Platte, Nebraska

Parkison, Sid
Broken Bow, Nebraska

Pierce, Leonard L.
Callaway, Nebraska

Pomplun, Ben
Broken Bow, Nebraska

Ramundo, Toni
Mitchell, Nebraska

Reno, Mrs. W. S.
Alliance, Nebraska

Rigney, Clara
Dayton, Wyoming

Rodine, Theodore E.
Gothenburg, Nebraska

Romans, Robert
Arnold, Nebraska

Runyan, Leota
Mason City, Nebraska

Schmitz, Wayne

Schroer, Mrs. Raymond
Kearney, Nebraska

Sheldon, Dick
Broken Bow, Nebraska

Simms, David H.
Mason City, Nebraska

Skelton, Bill
Broken Bow, Nebraska

Smets, Tex
Anselmo, Nebraska

Smith, Carl E.
Broken Bow, Nebraska

Swick, John
Lillian, Nebraska

Tobey, A. L.
Maxwell, Nebraska

Trimble, Mrs. Margaret C.
Kearney, Nebraska

Wait, Carl
Ansley, Nebraska

Whaley, John A.
Callaway, Nebraska

Wirsig, A. E.
Farmington, Iowa

Withers, Flora
Long Beach, California

Wood, Arthur
Callaway, Nebraska

Woodward, Bertha
Klamath Falls, Oregon

Worth W. A.
Almeria, Nebraska

People and Places